MW01382813

# ADVAN
# COMFORT, HEALING, AND JOY

*Comfort, Healing, and Joy is a caring guide that ushers us into claiming our birthright of inner and outer wholeness. It is a most excellent medicine for healing any sense of lack, limitation or unworthiness, and for stepping into the innate capacities of the human heart and spirit. Savor it!*

MICHAEL BERNARD BECKWITH
AUTHOR OF *SPIRITUAL LIBERATION~FULFILLING YOUR SOUL'S POTENTIAL*

*Dr. David Fox writes from the heart and shares his inspiration through personal stories, metaphors and useful tips. Reading this insightful book will guide you to live a richer and more meaningful life.*

DIANA DRAKE LONG
CO-AUTHOR OF *POWER & SOUL, CREATE THE BUSINESS & LIFE OF YOUR DREAMS*

*Reading Comfort, Healing and Joy is like listening to a wise and caring friend. Dr. David Fox has written a very readable guide for dealing with life's challenges and questions -- through practical and personal examples of triumph and inspiration.*

PATRICK LOSINSKI
EXECUTIVE DIRECTOR, COLUMBUS METROPOLITAN LIBRARY

*Dr. David Fox is deeply respected for his compassion and commitment to medicine. His words are honest and get to the core of. . . finding true happiness.*

DAVID P. BLOM
PRESIDENT AND CEO, OHIOHEALTH CORPORATION

*Buckle up. David gets real in this book! His use of compelling real life stories and practical tips about how to be happier and live a truly fulfilled life is raw and real. This is a down to earth, honest look at happiness and what it takes to live a fulfilled life, especially for those who struggle in this area. For those who think that happiness is just a pipedream or catch-phrase, this book will challenge your deepest, darkest, inner-most happiness gremlins!*

MEREDITH LIEPELT CEO, www.RichLifeMarketing.com

*Comfort, Healing and Joy is like having your personal life coach sitting in the same room with you. This book wraps its arms around you... an undertow of strength and motivation so when you finish the last page you are full of joy and peace.*

JANN MARKS
CHIEF NURSING OFFICER, RIVERSIDE METHODIST HOSPITAL, COLUMBUS, OHIO

*A straightforward journal that explores the attributes of an enjoyable life and shares simple mental tools for embracing a happier existence.*

KATHLEEN STARKOFF
CHIEF INFORMATION OFFICER, THE OHIO STATE UNIVERSITY

*The wisdom in Comfort, Healing, and Joy will naturally appeal to, and assist, those in pain, perhaps due to depression, anxiety or grief, but we all should take note of this book, regardless of how content we are with our lives. Dr. David Fox offers each of us guidance in finding our way to a more magnificent and fulfilled life.*

SARA SUKALICH, M.D.

*David Fox is a physician whose... success stems from high academic achievements always tempered with his own life experiences. This book distills, honestly and sympathetically, the problems he faced and helps others face. It is not a "how to" book but a "can do" book. For those principles, it is of extreme value.*

DR. BURTON R. SAIDEL

# COMFORT
# HEALING

AND

# JOY

## SECRETS TO LIVING A
## MAGNIFICENT LIFE

# DAVID FOX, M.D.

Love Your Life

LOVE YOUR LIFE PUBLISHING, INC.

Love Your Life Publishing, Inc.
7127 Mexico Road Suite 121
Saint Peters, MO 63376
www.LoveYourLifePublishing.com
publisher@LoveYourLifePublishing.com

ISBN: 978-1-934509-34-0
Library of Congress Control Number: 2010936606

Printed in the United States of America

Cover Design by MonkeyCMedia.com
Internal Design by: www.Cyanotype.ca
Additional Typesetting by: www.masterpagedesign.co.uk
Editing by Marlene Oulton and Gwen Hoffnagle

First Printing: 2010

# CONTENTS

## JOY

# DEDICATION

If not for you, this book would never be.

# Acknowledgements

First and foremost, I wish to thank the Source of all life's teachings. I am here only to deliver a message but I, myself, am not the message; I am simply the messenger. In the four months it took for these words to pour forth from my soul, I knew all along that I had "help."

I am grateful for all those who have come before me to leave their mark on the world through their generous gifts of wisdom that I was drawn to latch onto.

I am grateful for those I love most dearly, as I've taken you on some interesting journeys, always to return home again. You have helped nurture me, sustain me, and comfort me through feast and famine. You know who you are!

I am grateful for the vicissitudes of life that have blessed me, from the sublime beauty of a newborn's first cry to the grim wasteland that has on occasion enveloped me with a sadness that has brought me to my knees. I have needed them all in order become more and more of this person I was always meant to be.

I am thankful for the opportunity to welcome Diana Long into my life. Diana is a beautiful spirit and personal coach who has shared with me her uncanny ability to expose the heart of a matter, guiding me to *wait* and *allow* — rather than forge ahead boldly — as she helped me scatter seeds in the fertile soil of that creative space that resides deep within.

I am thankful for the blessing of Marlene Oulton, my original editor, whose keen eye for detail was matched by her generous enthusiasm and encouragement (i.e., hand-holding) to bring this project to fruition.

I am thankful for the gifted team of devoted professionals I was lucky enough to assemble for publishing, marketing, and designing this book — Lynne Klippel, Penny Sansevieri, Jeniffer Thompson, Julio Pompa, Anna Bobro, Gwen Hoffnagle, Sarah Barrie and Peter Barlow. I have genuinely and thoroughly enjoyed working with all of you!

Thank *you*, dear reader, for joining me as we stroll hand-in-hand together through each page. This book was written for you, after all, and if not for you, this book would never be.

# INTRODUCTION

The purpose of this book is simple and clear: to help you, dear reader, deepen your sense of meaning and fulfillment with life so that you naturally greet each morning with an emphatic "yes" to the day that is about to unfold.

Who am I to set such an ambitious goal for you?

In order to answer that question, I have no good option but to share with you certain private pieces of my past. To be honest, the mere thought of revealing some of my most deeply guarded secrets to the whole world makes me woefully uncomfortable. As you read on, though, you will understand and appreciate why I chose to make this sacrifice.

What began as a fairly typical bout of adolescent depression evolved into a lifelong search for the truth – my truth – that pitted me against my inner demons and culminated in a unique display of personal triumph. Coming face to face with the realization that my emotional cards were stacked against me, I decided then and there at the ripe old age of 17 that I wasn't going to take this depressive streak lying down; instead, I resolved to re-shuffle the deck. Having steeled myself for the long-term pursuit of meaning and fulfillment – however long it took didn't matter —- I succeeded gloriously in transforming my emotional fate in a fashion nothing short of spectacular.

At the age of 46, I was called upon by a subtle yet powerful force deep within me to write this book… correction… *this book practically wrote itself!…* to share with countless seekers of a beautiful life the spiritual, psychological, and emotional "pearls of wisdom" I have discovered on my journey.

I have written down these words as a guide to those kindred spirits who seek to squeeze every bit of juice out of life they can muster during the brief period of time they are given to occupy a part of this earth. Unless you are blessed with great genes *and* good fortune, life can be a struggle a little or a lot of the time. No matter where your life has taken you to this point, I believe that by the time you finish reading these pages, you will experience much more of the happiness that you deserve, now and in the future.

This is how my journey began:

*I was 17 years old. Raised in a middle-class family, with three siblings, a single set of parents and one dog, my life resembled that of plenty of other kids my age. My early childhood was basically a happy one, but over a period of just a few months during the later part of my teenage years, I found myself trapped in a deep depression.*

*This "A student" could barely get out of bed. I hated my life. I hated myself. Each new day was unbearable. My grades went down drastically, but I didn't even care. The college to which I had already been accepted threatened to rescind their offer if I didn't get my act together and turn my grades around. I didn't care about that prospect either. Nothing, literally nothing, I tried on my own could make me feel better.*

*I sought help through therapy. Finally after many months had gone by, I began to feel somewhat better, but still lived uncomfortably on the precipice of an emotional abyss. Vestiges of depression lingered on, waxing and waning day after day, month after month, year after year. To say the least, I was discouraged, often thinking "What is wrong with me? I must be defective… diseased… unhelpable."*

*Thankfully, I was congenitally blessed with one attribute in my personality that was pervasive enough to propel me forward in search of answers in spite of my pain. It turned out to be critical to my success in escaping the grip of seemingly endless despair. This one element that I had always possessed enabled me to trudge on in search of the wisdom that held the answers to life's questions: dogged persistence. I just would not — no, could not — quit. "Come hell or high water, I will find my way out of this damn depression," I told myself. And I did.*

Depression, for those who have experienced it, is an awful, nasty illness. I remember those early years well. They were sheer hell for me. I took notes, lots of notes. "Someday," I thought, even as a young man, "I will teach others how I escaped the clutches of depression, so that they perhaps will not have to endure as many of the hardships and heartaches that I did."

What I didn't realize at the time was that depression would once again rear its ugly head years later and yet again after many more years had passed. After many failed attempts to deny the truth to myself, and certainly to others, I finally arrived at the inescapable and painful conclusion that through nature or nurture, or some combination of both, I was prone to live in a state of unhappiness. However unfair this might have seemed, I was not born with what I call the Happy Gene, my metaphor for the natural tendency that some people have toward feelings of well-being and that hard-to-define word called *happiness*.

Throughout my life, I have personally observed numerous individuals that seem to naturally wake up every day singing "Zip-a-Dee-Doo-Dah." These are the folks that have never picked up a self-improvement book or tape, have never seen a counselor, and have trouble understanding why some people don't share their zest for life. These are the people who have won the genetic lottery and might not even realize it. In this one important area, I was not so blessed.

Once I realized that emotional well-being did not come naturally to me, I took this as a call to action, having decided rather emphatically that I would never settle for a life of despair. "Come hell or high water," became my personal mantra to overcome this hard-wired tendency and exhibit great sway over my emotional destiny. It hasn't always been easy. In fact it has been downright painful at times, but then again, I ask what my life would have been like had I *not* taken the actions I took to alter my fate. I don't think I want to contemplate the answer to that.

What you are now holding in your hands is a vehicle for sharing with you the secrets of life I have learned over the past 30 years that have enabled me to escape, more than once, the throes of depression. I want to help you use this knowledge to enhance your ability to lead a meaningful, fulfilling, and yes, often happy life, punctuated by moments of intense joy, gratitude, and beauty.

These words embody a distillation of my personal life experiences combined with those precious insights garnered from hundreds of books and tapes encompassing a disparate group of subjects including philosophy, psychology, Neuro Linguistic Programming (NLP), hypnosis, business, martial arts, spirituality, creativity, intelligence, meditation, writing, and self-improvement. Fortunately, you don't have to invest years of your time to read these same books and listen to these same tapes like I did, and you and I certainly cannot undergo the same life experiences. You have before you a tremendous shortcut — a ridiculously easy-to-read collection of simple truths that will lead you on your own path to self-discovery very quickly.

The book is organized into three sections that together comprise the fundamental elements of what I have found are vital to living a profoundly meaningful life. The **Comfort** section describes a number of foolproof ways in which you will learn to soothe yourself, especially when you find stress or anxiety getting in your way. **Healing** represents practical how-to ways of kicking the mental habits that can get you into a rut and keep you there. **Joy** is the reward you will experience once you have "primed the pump" with all the *soothing* and *healing* you have done to remove the barriers to emotional freedom.

Each chapter begins with a metaphor or observation from everyday life and ends with a virtual recipe for how you can apply the central message in your own unique way. Certain chapters could have easily fit into more than one section, so I simply made an arbitrary decision based on what I felt flowed the simplest. The order in which you read the chapters is usually not important, so simply choosing a chapter at random to read should work out well for most parts of the book.

I caution you to be flexible and open-minded in utilizing the material contained in this book. The cornerstone of my approach is to *try what works.* Just because I might have found a certain concept to be extremely valuable in my life does not mean that the same one will resonate with you. That's fine. I don't believe in a "one-size-fits-all" answer for every person or for every problem. Moreover, sometimes a particular approach will work on Monday, but not on Tuesday. That doesn't mean you should toss it out of your repertoire of tools. It simply means you should try something else on Tuesday. The more options you keep at your disposal, the better. You should know that I have practiced what I preach, having personally heeded the wisdom of each core message and applied it for my own great benefit.

It is my sincere hope that you will gain as much value in your life from these ideas as I have in mine. While my aspirations are lofty, my expectations are much more modest. If only *one idea* in this book imparts a subtle shift in your long-term state of well-being, I will consider this book a smashing success — easily worth the price you paid... and I hope you see it that way too!

# COMFORT

*"When I saw that rage was vain*
*And to sulk would nothing gain,*
*Turning many a trick and wile*
*I began to soothe and smile."*

WILLIAM BLAKE

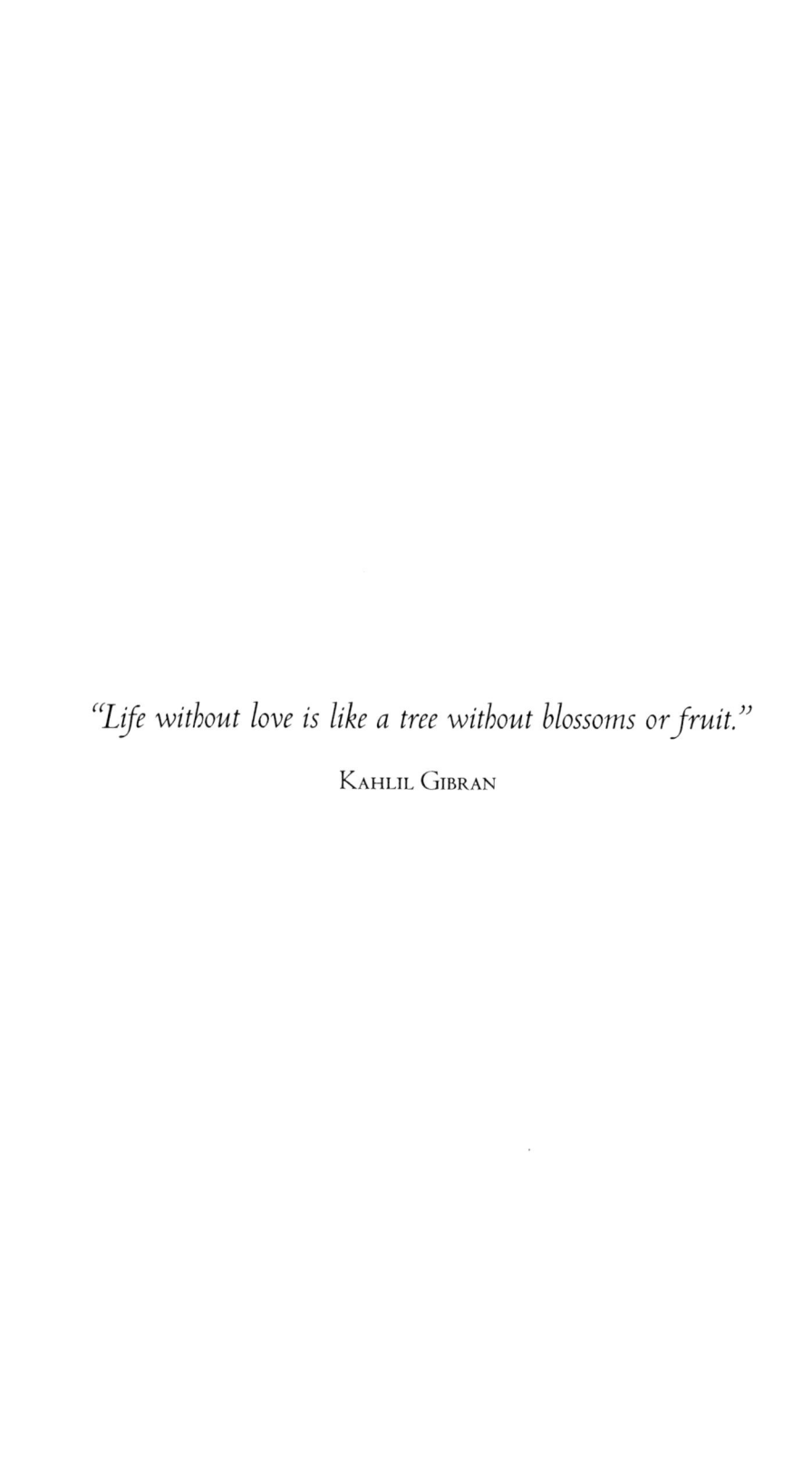

*"Life without love is like a tree without blossoms or fruit."*

Kahlil Gibran

# SEE YOURSELF
# THROUGH THE EYES OF LOVE

Contrary to what we insist on telling ourselves, we cannot "know" the world directly, as it truly exists in reality, because "reality" is different for all of us. Our perceptions of the world are colored by the unique lens — like a pair of glasses — through which our experiences are filtered. The lens, in turn, is formed from our personality, life experience, cultural upbringing, brain chemistry, belief system, values, and surely a whole host of other factors. While our subjective "maps" of the world may *approximate* reality, we would do well to recognize that what is true for us doesn't necessarily represent what is true for another human being. If you don't believe me, turn on the news someday to listen to how pundits on opposite sides of the political spectrum portray the same issue in vastly different terms.

The classic movie drama *Twelve Angry Men* speaks to the extreme biases each of us has in drawing interpretations from the same set of facts. In this film, set in the 1950s, an indigent minority youth is charged with murdering his father. Eleven members of the all-white jury are convinced of his guilt, and are ready to deliver a verdict that would send him to the electric chair. One juror who looks at the same set of facts defends a different point of view, and spends the rest of the film chipping away at the preconceived judgments of the other jurors, until the defendant is finally acquitted.

In the same way that our interpretation of the outside world is a product of our external lens, our inner world of thoughts and feelings is governed by an internal lens through which we see ourselves. This internal lens is our self-image. If we were to spend just a few seconds picturing ourselves as inferior or worthless, our gut reaction toward ourselves at that moment would be swift and forceful: we would feel terrible. On the other hand, when we see ourselves in a favorable light, we feel confident and secure. Even when we've not behaved at our best, we feel much more charitable toward ourselves when viewed through the bright, colorful lens of a positive self-image than through the dark dreariness of a negative one.

Some people were exposed early on in life to frequent criticisms and negative judgments, leaving them feeling like they're *never good enough*, or otherwise *incomplete* in some way. Over and over again throughout their lives they re-play that critical voice in their heads, generating the feeling of being inadequate each and every time they do. That inner voice can be so automatic and so subtle, a person might not even be conscious of hearing it at all. Even high achievers – perhaps that is *why* they are high achievers – can suffer from a poor self-image, leading them on a quenchless thirst for proving themselves worthy of validation from others over and over again. The trouble is they simply see themselves through the eyes of the harsh critic that resides within their minds, and they don't like who and what they see. If this is true for you, even sometimes, if not more often, there is another way.

Think of someone right now who loves you deeply and without conditions, in other words, for no particular reason at all. This person may be alive, and a part of your life, or they could have passed on long ago. If you can't think of anyone, that's alright, too. Just ask yourself what it would be like if someone *did* love you deeply and unconditionally, even if they're *not* in your life at this time.

In your mind's eye, step inside that person now. That's right, place yourself inside of them, and while you are there, see yourself through *their* eyes, the same eyes that hold a deep love for you. Notice how it feels when you picture yourself through the lens of unconditional love. If you could speak to yourself through this person, how affectionate would this loving voice sound to you? What would this caring voice say to you? How charitable would it be?

Now suppose you were *down* on yourself about something, whether you honestly feel you deserve it or not. How different do you think it would feel to see yourself from the point of view of this loving soul whose tender embrace is always with you? Wouldn't it feel a wee bit different than it would through the eyes of the inner critic who has judged you so harshly?

Try this the next time you are viewing yourself unkindly: Take out a blank piece of paper and write out a 5-minute dialogue between that critical inner voice and the voice that belongs to the one who sees you through those loving eyes. Write down the nastiest attack against you that the Harsh Critic can muster, using name-calling, trash talking, no-holds barred ugliness. Then allow the one with the Loving Eyes to defend you like a mamma bear protecting her cub. What would she (or he, as the case may be) say on your behalf? Then go for a second round — attack and rebuttal — then a third, until the Harsh Critic is out of ammunition and the one with the Loving Eyes has the last word about you. Don't try to do this in your head!

*Harsh Critic: You're such a loser! Why would anyone want to put up with you? You might as well give up!*

*Loving Eyes: She surely has had her share of disappointments, and has made some ill-advised decisions, but she possesses many wonderful qualities, too, and has much to offer to the world. She might get slowed down from time to time, but giving up is not in her vocabulary. And for your information, she has had many friends in her lifetime.*

*Harsh Critic: Oh yeah, then why does she keep making the same mistakes over and over again? Doesn't she ever learn? She screws everything up.*

*Loving Eyes: You're absolutely right, she is human, and recognizing that fact as she does makes her even more authentic. Who are you to say she never learns? Only she knows how much she has gained from her experience. I have known her a long time, and I know her to be a beautiful soul who does the best she can with what she has been given.*

*Harsh Critic: Since when is she so wonderful? She has struggled with the same problems for years. Obviously there is something really wrong with her, like she's defective!*

*Loving Eyes: No one is defective! I don't know where you get your information from but she has been blessed with talents and capabilities that might not be clearly visible to someone like you, someone who searches only for faults in others. The fact that you fail to see her many gifts says more about you than it does about her.*

The key to this very powerful exercise is to stay loving, stay honest, and stay humble. It's a good idea – vital actually – to have the one with Loving Eyes describe you as you are, warts and all, rather than ask her to portray you as someone that you're not. She accepts you as you are, in spite of all your imperfections – perhaps even *because* of them – yet she loves you anyway. Always!

See yourself through the eyes of love.

*"Ambition is so powerful a passion in the human breast, that however high we reach we are never satisfied."*

Henry Wadsworth Longfellow

# CAN YOU GIVE YOURSELF SOME APPROVAL?

Have you ever noticed that children can be very sensitive to being tickled? Sometimes just moving your hand toward their tummy can elicit giggles before any physical contact is made. A little anticipation is often all that is needed to get them laughing.

What has always fascinated me about tickling is the huge impact the mind has on this seemingly physical experience. Tickling is a mostly psychological experience. If you doubt that, go ahead and try to tickle *yourself*! Doesn't work very well, does it?

For many people, the effect of a compliment works in a similar way to being tickled. When other people stroke our egos, we stand a better chance of feeling good than when we try to praise ourselves. Hearing a hearty, "Nice work!" from a friend, co-worker, or loved one can boost our feelings of self-esteem like a wonder drug, whereas patting *ourselves* on the back by silently thinking the exact same words to ourselves seems to fall flat, assuming we even bother thinking about these words of praise in the first place.

Just because we can't tickle ourselves, does that mean we can't give ourselves praise for doing what we do, or being who we are? After all, wouldn't it be nice if we could boost our self-esteem on our own without always being at the mercy or whims of others?

As it turns out, we *can* compliment ourselves *and* feel good when we do. Maybe it is more gratifying to hear praise from others, but that doesn't mean that we have to wait for them to validate us each and every time in order for us to feel a sense of pride and satisfaction! If negative, twisted thoughts about ourselves can damage our self-esteem, it stands to reason that loving, accepting, and supportive thoughts about ourselves can boost it.

A huge barrier to rewarding one's self is the self-defeating belief that praising yourself is somehow "wrong" or "conceited" or even "immoral." If you believe this to be true, it's no wonder you have poor self-esteem. Whose voice is in your head anyway? Is it there to support you or tear you down? What would a supportive, loving person in your life say to you if they knew you believed you shouldn't praise yourself for one reason or another?

Try using what I call the "reverse" Golden Rule: Do unto yourself the way you would do unto others. This implies that if you would encourage a friend or loved one to feel good about themselves, you should certainly accept this same idea for yourself. Some very smart people often violate this basic rule.

In the case of some people, their dependency on the approval of others is so strong and all-encompassing that it actually sabotages their ability to feel good on their own. When the desire is so intense as to feel like a need, it's as if the person can *only* feel good when they hear praise from others, leading to feelings of insecurity and emptiness. This form of addiction is more like an addiction to food than to alcohol. With an alcohol addiction, the goal is usually to quit "cold turkey," since alcohol is not necessary for survival. With a food addiction, however, the objective obviously cannot be to *quit eating*. Such is the case with over-reliance on outside approval; while it's mentally healthy to ratchet down the extreme need for praise and recognition, nearly all of us need some semblance of validation by others to maintain a healthy emotional state. I, for one, wouldn't want to be the sort of person who didn't give a hoot what others think. The goal, then, is to find the right balance by turning down the need enough to leave room for lots of self-approval.

If you ever do find yourself having trouble basking in the glow of – for instance – something nice that you did for another person, check to see whether you are secretly counting on someone's approval as a pre-condition for feeling wonderful. If you didn't receive any positive strokes, that in no way means your deed didn't count. In fact, it counts just as much as if you received all the accolades in the world. Merely *recognizing* the self-defeating habit of over-emphasizing the need for approval is enough to at least take the edge off the craving. Once you stop seeking approval, you might just find that you seem to attract even more of it. Unsolicited approval tastes sweeter than pie!

Perhaps the biggest impediment to patting one's self on the back is due to that rather nasty word "but." This word is so short and innocent-looking. Who would think it has the power to tear people down in so many different ways? When you're not feeling good about yourself, look around hard for the word "but" in your self-talk, such as:

"I worked so hard, *but* I only placed second."

"I am nice to people, *but* they sometimes still don't like me."

"I'm doing better and better, *but* I've got a long way to go."

"I was able to stay strong for a while, *but* then my heart melted."

The word "but" erases everything that has come before it, leaving you to focus exclusively on the negative aspects of a situation. Your inner critic only hears, "I only got second place; " "They simply don't like me;" and "I've got a long way to go." Whatever you did was just not good enough. It's no wonder people don't give themselves enough credit with destructive words like that lurking around in their head!

How can you diffuse "but?" It's fairly easy if you know the antidote.

The cure to stop using the word "but" is to replace it with the word "and." You might think that the difference between using "but" and "and" is so insignificant that they convey the same meaning. Think again. Unlike the situation with "but," when you switch to "and" you can keep both halves of the sentence rather than suffer the consequences of rendering the entire positive half meaningless.

"I worked so hard *and* I only got second place."

"I am nice to people *and* they still sometimes don't like me."

"I'm doing better and better *and* I've got a long way to go."

The worst case scenario is that by keeping both parts, you see both the positive and the negative aspects of it, which leaves you with a neutral feeling rather than a negative one as is the case when using "but."

The ultimate goal of this easy switch, however, is not to walk away feeling neutral. Even better than neutral, "and" opens the door to the possibility of dropping the negative half of the expression from our attention altogether. Unlike "but," which seems to compel us to ignore the positive half, "and" does just the opposite by giving us permission to ignore the negative half, in essence eliminating it.

"I work so hard."

"I am nice to people."

"I'm doing better and better."

As soon as you find yourself negating a worthy effort you have made or a good deed you have done, see if you can find a "but" lurking around somewhere, and when you do, immediately replace it with "and." Once you can focus squarely on your positive efforts, it's only a matter of pointing them out to yourself. When you're not burdened by "but," it's rather straightforward to say, "I did a nice job with this project."

Making positive statements to yourself might at first generate about as much excitement within you as tickling yourself. Fortunately, the more you practice giving yourself gentle pats on the back, the more this conscious habit becomes an unconscious, automatic one. Over time as you get used to this practice, hopefully you will find that some very pleasant feelings about yourself start to percolate on their own and rise up into your awareness without much, if any, effort on your part.

What kinds of positive thoughts can you think about yourself? Try these on for size:

"How nice that I went the extra mile for a friend today."

"Look how I put my best foot forward, even when I didn't feel like it."

"I was extra patient with people today and really listened more intently than I usually do."

The number of opportunities to pat yourself on the back is endless. Be creative. Be gentle. And no *trying* allowed. It should be easy and relaxed and must never become a chore.

What's great about fishing for nice things to say about yourself to yourself is that the rules of this kind of success do not depend on the *results* of your efforts, only on the *efforts* themselves. If you try and fail, you can still "celebrate yourself" for trying since you're no longer saying, "I did it, *but it failed.*" It simply becomes, "I did it. I did it. I did it." You get credit for the *doing.* External success, therefore, becomes the *icing* on the cake rather than the cake itself!

There are some things you can do to turn positive thoughts about yourself into wonderful feelings! Isn't that really what you are after?

Have you ever noticed yourself *dwelling* on what you consider to be past mistakes? You think, "I messed up," and then you feel kind of bad about it, but you don't stop there. You repeat it to yourself over and over again until you've gotten yourself whipped into a frenzy to the point where you're feeling really awful. If this type of thinking goes on too long it can snowball, and become obsessive. If you have ever noticed how negative feelings can spin around inside of you, then you can appreciate how this exact same process can work to your advantage on the flip side, where dwelling on positive thoughts about yourself can create the spinning around of some really nice feelings inside of you which last *long after* the actual thoughts or words that generated the good feelings in the first place.

By *dwelling* on a positive thought over and over again in your mind, whether visualizing or not, you can really start to glow on the inside. You can begin to appreciate those good feelings rotating inside of you. The more you comfortably dwell on your positive thoughts, the faster the wheel spins, until it turns virtually all by itself. It'll eventually slow down and stop spinning, but once you know how to get it going again, you'll feel much more in charge of your emotional state.

Here is an easy technique to help get you going with this process. Write down on paper all the recent personal efforts or gains you have made for which you deserve some credit, regardless of whether or not they ultimately panned out in your favor. This exercise has no formal rules other than to pick things that you're truly proud of: your recent good deeds, inspired effort, personal triumphs, or whatever else you would like to add to fill up your tank of love for yourself. Experiment with using "I" versus "you" to describe yourself, and pick whichever one feels more natural. It should never be a chore to be done on a schedule. It is just another way of caring for yourself that promotes feelings of inner peace and harmony. Here is an example:

*"This week you have gone above and beyond the call of duty! You helped two friends move, bought a baby gift for another, and baked brownies for the fundraiser. Though you*

*pigged out a little on Sunday, you worked out in the morning, even though you didn't sleep as long as you'd hoped. You turned down the offer for a new committee, knowing that you had enough on your plate. You did all this and still found time to take your evening walks around the pond that you enjoy so much."*

Now that I've made my case for taking pleasure in your efforts, I have a very pleasant surprise for you...

You can even give yourself some love for no particular reason at all!

In your mind, simply ask yourself: "Can you give yourself some approval?" Think to yourself the word "yes" as you exhale through your nose. Spend a few moments asking repeatedly, for more and more approval – "Can you give yourself some *more* approval?" – and answer the same way each time, with a slow "yes" as you breathe out through the nose. Try closing your eyes when you do this.

In the event you don't feel that the answer "yes" is true for you, just relax, and ask yourself this question instead: "Wouldn't it be lovely if I *were* able to give myself some approval?" Go ahead and think "yes" as you release a calm breath slowly through your nose. And as you ask yourself this question a few more times, notice how wonderful it can feel to give yourself approval whenever you would like, without needing to justify it to anyone, including you...

Can you give yourself some approval?

*"By letting it go it all gets done. The world is won by those who let it go. But when you try and try. The world is beyond the winning."*

Lao Tzu

# Create Emotional Space Between You and Your Problems

One chilly, winter Sunday afternoon, I found myself doing what I often love to do: making soup. My favorite kind is homemade; thick with hearty vegetables, and as hot as I can stand it. After washing, peeling, and chopping all the vegetables and roots that lend the soup their rich flavors, I add the water and allow the simmering heat to perform its magic for the next few hours. As the house fills up with the savory aroma of this bubbling concoction, it's time to take my first careful taste: ouch, too hot! — another burn to the roof of my mouth. Why don't I ever learn? If I had waited for that spoonful of soup to cool for just a few moments, a blister would not be forming followed by the soreness and numbness that goes along with the sloughing of tissue. If only I had *put it off* a little longer.

Usually I am pretty adept at putting things off. I love to put off doing the dishes, and I usually put off taking out the trash. And though I almost always get to it eventually, I frequently put off exercising. Procrastination is a part of my life. Wait until you read, in just a few moments, how a smidgeon of procrastination can change your life for the better!

Did you ever notice that whenever something bothers you from the past or the future, the "bother" is always **here right now** in the *present* moment? When you become preoccupied with what *was*, or concerned about what you think *will be*, perhaps you get a bloated, heavy feeling, or some other physical sensation that makes you uncomfortable and sometimes downright ill. You can talk about what is bothering you, trying to push it out of your mind; you can fight against it; ignore it, or try to control it. Sometimes any of these strategies are appropriate and effective, but when they cease to be either, there is another choice for dealing with a thought or feeling that is bothering you.

You can learn to Let It Go.

Letting go sounds good in theory, and it would seem on the surface to make sense, but you would be right to ask the question, "How exactly am I to go about doing this? How can I just let my problems go?"

The answer is that you don't let your real problems go. What you can let go of is the negative *thought or feeling* that gets *attached* to the problem. Sometimes just the thought or feeling *is* the problem, and if you let that go, there actually is no real problem left to worry about.

The short answer to "How can I do this?" is that there are many, many things that you can do to try to free yourself from the particular *emotional charge* that is bothering you at any given point in time. Some methods will work for you splendidly; others might never seem to help you, while still others will work at certain times, but not at others. Once you're caught in the grip of a powerful negative emotion, an *immediate* remedy may not be so simple, as the negative feeling might already be spinning around too furiously inside of you to stop it. The key then is to try to catch yourself in the early stages before the negative emotion has you in a stranglehold.

As soon as you recognize that you are flirting with a bothersome thought or feeling that could get out of hand, ask yourself the following questions:

(1) "Is it *possible* for me to put this off until later?"

In other words, can you put that thought or feeling on the back burner for a few moments since *now is not a good time* to entertain it? Answer silently to yourself. Your answer will either be "yes" or "no." Even though you would like to answer unequivocally "yes," it is important to answer this question honestly. Therefore, if the answer is not "yes," then it is "no," and where does that leave you? Not much better off. There is a third choice, an elegant solution, and a beautiful alternative to "no." The alternative to "yes" is "not yet."

"Not yet" is a powerful reminder of hope, a far cry from the cut-and-dried answer of "no." "Not yet" implies it *may* be possible to wait on giving attention to a bothersome thought or feeling, but you're not convinced that you can do it, and that's alright for now.

Here's a delicious twist that will enhance the pleasantness of this exercise. Time your answers with your breathing. When you wish to mentally answer "yes," wait until your body signals that it's time to breathe out, then enjoy the relaxation as you slowly exhale through your nose while you think of the word "yes." If you wish to answer "not yet," mentally say to yourself the word "not" as you inhale, followed by "yet" as you exhale slowly through your nose. Discover how timing your answers with your breathing can add a whole new relaxing dimension to this exercise.

(2) "Am I *willing* to put this off till later?"

This means that if it were possible to hold off for a little while, are you willing to *allow* that to happen? Is your answer "yes" or "not yet?"

(3) "What would it be like if I could let it go for good?"

Using a simple word or sentence, what would your life be like if you had this option of releasing it forever? Just let your mind be easy and allow your imagination to wander and see what pleasant possibilities emerge.

To review, anytime you have a disturbing or annoying thought or feeling happening *right now*, try asking yourself these questions:

"Is it possible for me to *put this off*?"

"Am I willing to put this off?"

"What would it be like if I could let it go for good?"

If you feel lighter and less bothered before you reach the end of the questions, by all means go ahead and quit this exercise. You are done! If, on the other hand, you find that one round of the questions leads to partial relief or none at all, try repeating the questions right away to see if repetition helps you chip away at the negative emotional charge. Go through these questions *up to three times* if necessary. If this method doesn't work for you satisfactorily the first time, you can always come back to it later and try it again.

Very simple technique, isn't it? The best part is that you needn't worry that you're being irresponsible for neglecting your real problems. If the situation truly calls for your attention, coming back to it when you're in a better mood will render you much more effective at dealing with it successfully than if you try to tackle it when you're coming from a negative energy state.

Create emotional space between you and your problems.

*"I destroy my enemies when I make them my friends."*

# MAKE PEACE WITH THE ENEMY WITHIN

It never feels good for me to think bad thoughts about another person. On those occasions when I have done this, I generally feel uncomfortable within myself, even if the other person has acted poorly. So, I try to keep disparaging opinions about others to a minimum. Yet, clearly there have been a few individuals I haven't particularly meshed with, and in rare cases I have regarded their behavior as so caustic that despite my best efforts to be charitable, I eventually reached the point of disliking them deeply. So much so that I found my attitude toward them became "dug in" and hardened in stone over time. I know I have finally given up trying to adapt to the disparity between us when I reach the conclusion that I simply don't like them. For the purposes of this discussion only, and not because I genuinely portray these people as such, you could say that they have become my enemies.

When we habitually do not see eye to eye with a person, we might decide to end our relationship with them. After all, if they are causing us to feel stressed, why should we keep them in our lives? The trouble is that such people are sometimes included in a "package deal," attached at the hip to someone we deeply care about. This *problem person* could be a friend of a friend, a relative of ours, or the spouse of someone we love. Therefore, even if we don't want to be gracious, we find ourselves inviting them into our home anyway.

How do you deal with someone that bothers you? Available options include running from them, fighting against them, or ignoring them, right? What if I told you that running and fighting just made your nemesis stronger and more capable of making your life miserable? Ignoring them, therefore, *seems* to be your only remaining choice. Or is it? If someone suggested that you make peace with your adversary, you would probably shake your head and say something like, "Yeah, right!" or "Fat chance!"

Let's pretend that your opponent is an *annoying thought or emotion* instead of a live human being, one that you definitely want to get rid of, but don't quite know how to do so. You have tried ignoring this bothersome thought, but can't seem to shake it. You have fought against it, but that just made it "mad," allowing it to strengthen its grip over you. You've even tried running away from this troublemaker by distracting yourself with activities, and for a while that might seem to work. Yet, it always seems to show up on your doorstep when you least expect it.

What would it be like if you could embrace that troubling thought or feeling? "Ridiculous," you might say. "What a dumb idea!" You're probably right, but before you reject this idea, I'd like to ask you a hypothetical question: What would your life be like right now if you *could* welcome that painful thought or feeling into your environment rather than avoiding it? (I know that you can't, but how would you feel if you could?) At first, this idea might seem kind of crazy, and it is, but each time you *play with* this "outrageous" possibility, the more you just might find that the enemy — the challenging thought or emotion — can begin to soften... and soften some more, and even more.

Facing the villain rather than running away involves four stages: Love, Embrace, Welcome, and Accept, in that order.

The first question to ask yourself is, "Can I allow myself to *Love* this thought or feeling?"

If you can answer "Yes," congratulations! You have made peace with the enemy within. I don't mean a half-baked, "Yes, now please pass the potatoes" kind of *yes*. I'm talking about a truly heartfelt "Yes!" — no ifs, ands, or buts attached. If you can't yet say it with that sort of conviction, then the better answer for now is, "Not yet."

If you answered "Not yet," move on to "If I can't love this thought, can I at least *Embrace* it?"

If the answer is, "Not yet," then say, "If I can't embrace this thought, can I at least *Welcome* it?"

If "Not yet," then respond with, "If I can't welcome it, can I at least *Accept* it?"

If you get to Accept without a "Yes," but still a "Not yet," what then?

"Not yet" is not a failure! It is a powerful alternative to "No." It means there is a chance to make peace, if not now then in the future. When you answer "Not yet," you are acknowledging that there is always hope. Merely having some hope, a possibility, is enough to soften the emotional ties that bind you to this thought or feeling. Each time you soften this connection, you weaken it, moving you closer and closer to "Yes."

So, keep asking "Can I allow myself to Love — Embrace — Welcome — Accept…?"

Each time you can get a real "Yes!" to any of these questions, you can begin to notice how its emotional grip over you has dissipated to a degree that it has lost its power to bother you, a sure sign that the process of letting go completely is inevitable. In essence, you have invited the enemy into your home, where it visits peacefully in your presence until it decides it has no more business there, gets up, and quietly leaves, never to return.

Love, Embrace, Welcome, and Accept.

Make peace with the enemy within.

*"Keep high aspirations, moderate expectations, and small needs."*

William Howard Stein

# GRADE YOUR OWN
# REPORT CARD

When I was growing up, grading in school was very simple: A, B, C, D, F. Everyone knew what each letter meant, and no one ever wanted a D or F. Nowadays grades are not so clear-cut. Some schools still use letter grades, but with added pluses and minuses; some use percentage grades; still others have abandoned traditional letter grades altogether. While the use of letter grades doesn't tell the whole story about a student's achievement and performance, the simplicity of its use still seems alluring to me.

In areas of our lives outside of school, we can also assign letter grades. The parts of our lives to which I am referring are:

- Inner life
- Love life
- Family life
- Friends
- Work
- Community

**Inner life:** The relationship we have with ourselves encompasses our mind, spirit, and body. How do you treat yourself? Are you generally accepting of your own imperfections, or do you beat yourself up a lot? Do you engage in activities that nurture your spirit, such as praying, meditating, or yoga? Do you treat your body as a temple of the soul, replenishing it with nourishing food and drink, or have you let yourself go through adopting an unhealthy lifestyle? Do you seek to achieve and maintain some modicum of physical conditioning?

**Love life:** How is your love life? Are you involved in a relationship, and if so, to what extent is it meeting your emotional, spiritual, and physical needs? Does your partner support you or do they tear you down? How do you treat them?

**Family life:** Do you have a family or people in your life that treat you like you're a member of their family? How would you characterize the state of your interactions with them? Are they supportive of you, and you of them?

**Friends:** What about your social life? Do you have at least a friend or two that you can count on to be there when you need them, and they on you?

**Work:** Do you enjoy your work or whatever it is that you do during the day? Is it satisfying to you? Do you manifest joy and purpose in your work?

**Community:** Are you involved in any charitable groups or causes? How do you contribute to the world outside of yourself and your inner circle? Do you give back to the world at least as much as you receive, provided you are in a position to give?

What I am interested in is not the content of these various aspects of your life, but rather the letter grade you would give each one if you had to assign yourself an A, B, C, D, or F. Are you one of the fortunate few whose entire life is running on all cylinders, and would give yourself straight As? Do you have mostly Bs and Cs? Are there any Ds or Fs?

The performance in one area of your life – your love life, for instance – can have a profound effect, both positive and negative, on all other areas. This is both good and bad news. The good news is that a grade of A in one area can raise you from a C to an A or B in another. On the other hand, a grade D or F in one place can drag your grades down in others. For instance, take job performance. Severe stress or dissatisfaction on the job can bleed into your family life if you are preoccupied with your work day when you return home. Conversely, problems at home can interfere with your performance and satisfaction at work.

Because one part of our life can cause a seismic shift in another, we can be fooled into focusing our efforts to troubleshoot our stress in the wrong direction! We may falsely tell ourselves that our troubles lie primarily in one area, when the true "heart" of the matter actually lies in another. The real problem could be something we are avoiding having to deal with for one reason or another. So, the area that has gotten dragged down as an innocent bystander becomes a *sideshow* that we mistakenly focus on for repair, when in reality we really want to avoid confronting the true source of our aggravation!

I doubt anyone would be satisfied with Ds and Fs in any area. That's pretty much a given. Just being willing to assign a failing or near-failing grade tells us that we know when we're having trouble in certain parts of our lives, and those areas are easily identified as ones needing some attention.

I don't know about you, but I'm personally not satisfied with many, if any, Cs. To me a C signifies mediocrity, and I would like to believe I have higher standards for myself than to readily accept a ho-hum performance in any facet of my life.

On the other hand, while I would like to earn straight As, (and I admittedly strive to do so), that goal is not always achievable. Plus the price I would have to pay to reach and maintain this level could be too high in terms of stress and effort; I just might not be willing to work so hard on everything at once.

My prescription for balancing life's various domains is to distinguish between aspirations and expectations. You can choose to *aspire* toward lofty goals in any or every part of your life, even straight As if you'd like, yet simultaneously *expect* of yourself nothing higher than Bs in anything. That way you don't have to suffer in the feelings of failure or mediocrity, and you don't have the pressure of "overachieving" all the time either. "Bs or better" is attainable, sustainable, and a high enough benchmark for excellence for those of us who want to lead fulfilling lives and are willing to put forth the effort to make it so.

Grade your own report card.

*"Sorrow is one of the vibrations that prove the fact of living."*

Antoine de Saint-Exupery

# Put Up With a Few Unpleasant Feelings

One of my favorite desserts to bake is banana bread with chocolate chips. Whenever I make it, people wonder what I add that makes it taste so good. The secret ingredient is... I have no secret ingredient. It's how I choose the bananas that make it taste so sweet and delicious.

Bananas in the grocery store are often firm, bright yellow fruits tinged with a green hue that screams out, "Not yet!" After a couple days of ripening and when the green finally disappears, this perfect looking fruit appears ready to eat. Not for me and certainly not for my bread! What I am looking for are those bananas that appear to be just past their prime; the ones with the big brown spots on the skins that bear little resemblance to the bright shiny ones I brought home from the store. I want the ones that remorsefully declare, "Sorry, dear, you're a little too late." Despite the brownish peel, and the often bruised and mushy exterior, it is this "uglier" version of the original that contains the sweetest pulp. And so it is with people, too.

Let me ask you a question: Given a choice, who would you rather hang out with? Someone who appears perfect in every way and acts as if they know this is so, or someone who is a transparent combination of both good and not-so-good qualities, freely admits their own flaws, yet approves of you in spite of yours? I don't know about you, but I would be much more endeared to the one that acts like a good old-fashioned, down-to-earth, flawed human being than one that wears a godlike facade.

When a well-meaning individual tries to be flawless and finds they can't achieve this ideal, a gap forms between where they really are – their true selves – and where they think they *should* be. When the gap is large and they focus their attention on it, they feel like they are *never good enough.* The wider the gap, the worse they are liable to feel about themselves.

This principle applies to one's sense of emotional well-being as well.

Let's assume that aside from some extremely unusual people, everyone has times when they mull over negative thoughts and encounter negative emotions. Feeling "blue," anxious, insecure, empty, depressed, angry, jealous or resentful are sobering states of human reality that are sometimes unavoidable, even for the naturally happiest individuals. These are the "brown spots" of human emotions that make us human. Virtually no one is happy 100% of the time!

A number of people accept these unpleasant episodes as a normal and temporary part of life, whereas others view such events as signs of personal defeat and intolerable fallibility. The trouble is that when we label our negative thoughts and feelings as "bad," as in we *shouldn't* experience them because to do so means we're somehow defective, we worsen and prolong our misery. In effect we create what I call a "double whammy."

A single whammy is when we feel bad in the first place. Left alone and judged as part of life, we usually get over these emotional ordeals fairly quickly and thoroughly. The double whammy is when we not only feel bad, but *we feel bad for feeling bad.* In other words, we feel bad *because* we feel anxious, *because* we feel depressed, *because* we feel angry. We might even compare ourselves to the "other bananas" because they don't have the exact same brown spots as we do. It's as if we want to dodge our negative emotions at all costs, thus we beat ourselves up for feeling what we're feeling. This both worsens and prolongs the funk that we work ourselves into which can last for a long, long time until we feel "stuck" or helpless to move past it.

If this scenario applies to you, the answer to this dilemma is to accept your unique pattern of brown spots as *who you are.* When I say *accept,* I don't mean to *tolerate begrudgingly.* True acceptance means welcoming and embracing your blemishes. It means acknowledging the gap between your real and ideal emotional selves and being completely satisfied with the "real" you, not giving a hoot about the gap or what's on the other side.

The paradox is that once you give up questioning the legitimacy of your negative emotions and stop trying to run from them, you create the conditions for them to stop bothering you. Leftover thoughts of them may or may not hang around for a little while, but who cares? As long as these lingering thoughts aren't bothering you, you can live side by side with them in peace.

If you ever criticize yourself for feeling anxious or for experiencing some other disturbing emotion, instead of saying, "Here I go again. What's wrong with me? I shouldn't feel this way. I hate myself," try taking on this attitude: "I hate this feeling. It's unpleasant. I prefer that it pass me by like a dark cloud floating across the deep blue sky. But for right now, I give myself permission to feel this way. It is not my goal to eliminate all my negative emotions once and for all so that I can feel "happy" 100% of the time, as that will never happen. This too shall pass. It always does. In the meantime, I'm going to put my best foot forward and enjoy my life."

In your imagination, see yourself smiling and standing strong in the face of adversity, like a big, old oak tree bending in the fierce wind of a thunderstorm as it has many times before. What would it be like if you could accept negative emotions without reacting to them? Even if you believe you can't, how would it feel if you thought you *could*? Just imagine what that would be like if you could. How lovely would that be?

When you adopt this attitude and see yourself doing so, everything changes. You'll still feel crummy now and then like everyone else does, but it need not be attached to the neurotic thought that something is seriously wrong with you. By allowing yourself to feel bad, without self-criticism, you're immersing yourself in your humanity. Feeling bad is not only a by-product of being human; it can make you *feel* genuinely human. Now there's an idea you can wrap your arms around!

Put up with a few unpleasant feelings.

*"Nothing is too wonderful to be true."*

MICHAEL FARADY

# Tap Into Your Inner Wisdom

I'll never forget the first time I heard about atoms. I was in grade school when I learned that atoms were the tiniest particles that got together to form the building blocks for everything we see — chairs, lamps, trees, my own body — and even some things that we can't see, such as gases. Though I knew I didn't stand a chance of ever actually seeing one of these atoms, I accepted the fact of their existence in the world.

Later on in science class, I learned what atoms are made of: a central component called a nucleus, and an outer part that contains electrons which swirl around the nucleus. As an adult, I became intrigued with the rest of the atom, namely the empty space within them. The fact of the matter is, over 99.9% of an atom is empty space. Since you and I are made up of atoms, we are almost entirely composed of... nothing!

Next time you peer up into the night sky noticing the moon and stars, maybe some clouds, you might want to take notice of all the rest — the "nothing" that surrounds them. The vast majority of the universe, so far as we can tell, is full of *nothing*. Before you get too depressed, consider the possibility that there may be more to *nothing* — much more — than meets the eye. To put it another way, *nothing* might actually mean *something*.

Deep inside of all of us, there is a special place, an inner core, where *nothing* resides. We cannot observe this place called *nothing*, for that would require having thoughts and interpretations about this place, so we only know that we've visited there after the fact. *Nothing* is quiet, still, and timeless.

In everyday life, we spend so much of our time focusing our attention outward toward activity. We have chores to do, errands to run, bills to pay, and people who depend on us to meet their needs. Oftentimes we put our dreams on the back burner because we have neither the time nor the focus to attend to them. Someday, we tell ourselves, we'll make the time. Someday never comes.

One of the best decisions I ever made was to learn how to direct my attention inward for brief periods of time, in the direction of *nothing*. Much of the time spent on my voyage to *nothing* is consumed in the process of getting there. I know when I'm not there yet because I still have thoughts running through my head and *nothing* is devoid of thoughts. But after I've spent some time immersed in *nothing*, part of me knows — I cannot explain how — that I have been there.

Why do I want to spend some of my precious time, when I have so little of it to spare, taking a voyage to *nothing*? Because *nothing* is not nothing at all. Nothing is something wonderful, "too wonderful to be true," as scientist Michael Faraday once pointed out.

If atoms are 99.9% empty, why don't we fall through the chair every time we try to sit in it? Because there is more to *nothing* than just empty space. That space contains an invisible force, an energy that makes what appears to be nothing actually something quite magical.

I am not here to unravel the mysteries of the universe. I am unsure about the relationship between the nothingness that is observed in the physical world and the nothingness that I have bumped into when I've turned my attention inward. I don't understand the mechanism by which I am able to encounter the silent, still core within me that produces a feeling of oneness with the universe. I surely cannot explain with any degree of certainty how these encounters make me feel so energetic, creative, rested and relaxed, and *alive*. But they do. And I wish I knew why after having these experiences, food tastes sweeter, flowers appear more colorful, and the air smells fresher, but they do.

I am also not here to promote a particular worldview, religion, or vehicle for turning inward to experience the silence that is present inside of you, but I *am* here to implore you to find some method of journeying to your inner core that fits your style, so that you, too, can benefit from a heightened sense of well-being and an increased zest for life as I have.

Many years ago while in undergraduate school, I found myself in dire straights, feeling the effects of so much life stress that I contemplated taking some time off from college to pursue more modest goals than that of becoming a physician. During that period of time I came across a flyer on the wall of the student union stairwell that advertised a free lecture to promote a meditation technique that, among other benefits, lowered stress. Since nothing appeals to a poor college student more than the word "free," I jumped at the chance to learn more.

Ultimately I scraped together the money to learn to meditate, and my life has never been the same since. From the very first time I practiced this ancient technique, I could literally feel the stress beginning to melt away. I was hooked on this new elixir as a way of improving my mental health. Quickly getting on a path to feeling better enabled me to comfortably stay in school and graduate with high honors.

There are many forms of meditation you can learn. Some are religious in nature, others secular. Some are expensive, whereas others are free. Some are difficult at first as there is a learning curve to get past before becoming proficient, while others start working right away.

The form of meditation I chose to learn is Transcendental Meditation (TM). Popularized by The Beatles and numerous other celebrities over the years, many people have at least heard of it, and millions have received instruction on how to practice TM. In its basic form, the one I recommend, it is practiced for twenty minutes twice daily. It is easy to do, nearly effortless, and works quickly and effectively to give refreshment to the mind. Regular practice produces cumulative benefits such as reduced tension, increased restfulness, and heightened creativity.

I once read a quote that pretty much summed up my experience in life. To paraphrase, it said that prayer is "speaking" to God, while meditation is "listening" to God. If you believe in God or some other description of a Higher Power, perhaps the practice of meditation might resonate with you. Even if you don't believe in a Higher Power, meditation still works, as no belief of any kind is required.

One misconception I have heard is that meditation is some sort of mystical practice that requires one to "stop thinking" or "clear their mind," neither of which they feel they have the capability of doing. Nothing could be further from the truth! Meditation entails the opposite of control; it's a natural process of letting go.

You can easily locate a TM teacher (www.TM.org) or seek out a teacher of another form of meditation, yoga, or other stress-reduction techniques by searching the Internet. While I do believe that some forms of meditation are easier to practice and faster to achieve results from than others, I don't believe there's a singular path that everyone must take to find peace, as different practices appeal to different people. Find one that's right for you. Of all the steps I have taken to induce inner calm and unleash my creativity, one of the most powerful has been the practice of meditation.

Tap into your inner wisdom.

*"Prayer does not change God, but changes him who prays."*

SOREN KIERKEGAARD

# POUR YOUR HEART OUT TO THE UNKNOWABLE

I remember the time, as a young boy, when I was finally allowed to take my own bath. I developed a routine that was unique to me, and it went something like this: I would fill the tub with warm water and lie down on my back, with only my eyes, nose, and mouth exposed to the air. Then with the water still running, I pressed the button with my toe that converted the bath to a shower. Though my ears remained below the surface of the water, I could hear the muffled sounds of the water striking against the pool of water in which I lay, infusing me with a feeling both pleasant and soothing.

As I imagine this time again, it's as if I can still feel the inner peace below the surface of the water, where I could surrender to the loving warmth that permeated my body and calmed my mind. Below the surface was a place of Being, where time was suspended, a wonderful respite from all the Doings that existed above. After a while, once the heat began to dissipate from the water, and the skin covering my fingers shriveled up like a prune, I knew that I was clean — squeaky clean — and it was time to come back to reality, wrap myself in a soft, fluffy towel that gently caressed my skin, and put on my fresh pajamas.

Those baths became a ritual of sorts for me.

Nowadays I take a different kind of bath, one that doesn't take water yet leaves me feeling clean. It is a spiritual bath of the highest order. And like the kind I first took as a young boy, I know that to cleanse myself I must return to this special kind of bath again and again.

Consider immersing yourself in the penetrating, fortifying warmth of prayer. Wrap yourself in the love of the unknowable. Cleanse yourself at anytime as you wash away your troubles in the infinite bath of sweet surrender.

Pour your heart out through words spoken aloud, through thoughts uttered silently, or by way of pen and paper. Step outside your analytical mind that asks questions. Suspend judgment as to whether anyone is listening or not. Adopt the attitude that "this is good for me" whether you can understand why or not, and whether you receive any answers or not. And then pour out your heart completely, as there are no secrets between you and your Higher Power.

- Admit your shortcomings and insecurities.
- Confess your transgressions.
- Release your burdens.
- Plead for strength, healing, wisdom, and guidance.
- Rant and rave about the injustices of mankind and the pain and suffering that afflict the innocent.
- Send a healing request to friend and foe alike.
- Declare heartfelt gratitude for what "is" even in the midst of what "is not."
- Proclaim your deep love for the creator of the universe.
- Do not pray to have some wish delivered to your feet.
- Do not pray for outcomes that violate laws of nature.
- Do not *wait* to pray until only after you have unraveled the mysteries of the universe.

When prayer comes from the heart, there is no right way or wrong way. What matters only is *your* way. When you pray from the heart, when you merge with the infinite and empty your vessel through the intimate outpouring of all that is within you that begs to come out, you can yet again become cleansed of your worries as you wrap yourself in love.

Pour your heart out to the unknowable.

*"Breath is the bridge which connects life to consciousness, which unites your body to your thoughts."*

THICH NHAT HANH

# Breathe in the Rhythm of the Ocean Tide

Take a trip with me down by the sea, where the air smells of salt and the wind gently caresses your skin in just the right way. Watch as the last faint rays of the sun drop down beyond the distant horizon, presenting the initial cusp of darkness that soon fills the sky. Listen to the ebb and flow of the ocean tide as it floods the tiny grains of sand with its bubbly swirls of foam that spread slowly toward your feet, only to recede quickly back toward the vastness of the sea. Back and forth…back and forth…in a rhythm governed by the mysterious pull of both sun and moon alike.

Just as the ocean tide speaks in its own natural rhythm, so, too, do we breathe in our own natural rhythm…back and forth…in and out. Breathing can be easy, fun and pacifying, especially if you know how to make it so. Let's explore a special way of breathing that you can do anywhere at anytime, that feels soothingly pleasant.

When I was a young boy, I used to check out my navel and wondered what its purpose was. No matter how much I studied it and compared it to that of others, I still didn't know what it was for. When I got older and finally solved that puzzle that had plagued me for years, I discovered that it was the remnant of my pre-birth attachment to my lifeline, namely my mother. I was relieved to solve this mystery. As an adult, I discovered a new purpose for the navel, and I would like to share it with you in just a moment.

When someone feels anxious and can't break the cycle of anxiety, a sense of helplessness and lack of control can take over, making them feel even worse. Bodily sensations can take on a life of their own in the form of tenseness, rapid heart rate, agitation, and countless other unpleasant experiences unfold. The best antidote for these annoying times is, of course, relaxation.

Telling someone who is caught in the web of anxiety or a full-blown panic attack to simply relax is a common practice. In my experience, the individual on the receiving end of this advice is usually ill-equipped to comply with this advice. A natural response, other than a frustrated, "Yeah, right!" would be, "That would be great, but how do I do that?"

So, I will not suggest that you simply "just relax." That would seem silly. Instead I'll show you one easy, very effective way to *at least* take the edge off that nervous energy, and possibly even transform you into a pleasant state of mind. Fortunately, this technique — actually it's a combination of two techniques — can be practiced by anyone, and when it does work to its fullest potential, *you begin to feel very calm.* The one caveat is, you can't just think about trying it for it to be effective — you actually have to do it.

Now back to the navel.

Much of our normal breathing is "chest breathing." We take in a breath and our chest rises. When we're anxious, not only do we breathe into the chest, we tend to take quick, shallow breaths. To change our physiology and counteract a negative emotional state, we can intentionally choose to change the way we breathe. Anyone can do this at anytime.

**Part I:** If you were to tie an imaginary string to the outside of your navel, and you asked some helpful imaginary force to pull on that string every time you breathed in, your belly would appear to fill up with air, as if a balloon were inside of it just underneath the skin. This "belly breathing" is the first component of this technique to relax.

Go ahead and try this for a few breaths. Breathe in through the nose, and in your mind's eye, allow your navel to be pulled outward by the imaginary string, as the balloon fills your belly. If this is brand new to you, you might want to place your open palm over your navel to directly experience the expansion and contraction with each breath.

**Part II:** Have you ever noticed how you feel when you sigh? Go ahead, try it. Take in a nice breath, and let it out slowly through your nose, like you're pretending to sigh. Notice that when you breathe out an *extended* breath, your body begins to settle down. Go ahead now and take in a nice, easy breath through your nose, and let it out even slower than it came in. The "extended breath out" is the second component of this soothing way of breathing.

**Part III:** All you have to do to relax your body in this easy, beautiful manner is to remember two simple things: breathe into the balloon underneath your navel and let it out slowly and comfortably through your nose.

It might be helpful sometimes to count as you breathe. With each breath in, silently count to 4, and with each breath out, count to 7 in your mind. I'm not talking about 4 or 7 seconds. I mean 4 and 7 "counts" at whatever pace is most comfortable for you.

A lovely feature of this method of relaxing is that it can be done anytime you feel the need or desire to relax and enjoy your breathing. I love having this experience in the morning while I'm still lying in bed, or at bedtime when I'm ready to drift off to sleep.

Breathe in the rhythm of the ocean tide.

*"We must act out passion before we can feel it."*

# ACT THE PART YOU WOULD LIKE TO PLAY

"It's better to look good than to feel good." This little catch phrase, used by actor Lorenzo Lamas and parodied by comedian Billy Crystal, is one that I take issue with. Personally I would rather feel good than look good, but we might just find something valuable in this saying. Is there a relationship between looking good and feeling good? You bet!

Have you ever known one of those people who seem to have been born with a perpetually sunny disposition? I have known a few. One such person was a woman I'll call Lisa, with whom I worked during my medical training. No matter what challenges came her way, Lisa invariably dealt with them in the most life-affirming way possible, seemingly always looking at the bright side. I used to joke that if you cut off her left arm she would thank you for leaving the other one intact! You could just "look" at her and tell she felt a deep sense of inner peace and joy most of the time.

Lisa "looked" happy most of the time. She smiled a lot, and her face had a glow that was hard to describe. Her voice was clearly audible and upbeat. She stood up straight, walked at a comfortable pace, made clear eye contact, and held her shoulders back as if she faced the world filled with self-confidence.

If you looked at my friend Lisa walking next to a person who was in a depressed mood, chances are you could tell them apart without being told which was which. This is not always the case, as a person who is feeling depressed can often successfully cover up the way they feel. But there can be signs:

- Their face is expressionless
- They look down toward the ground
- They walk slowly
- Their speech is slow or hushed
- They sigh often
- Their shoulders are hunched over
- Their breathing is shallow
- Their hair, hygiene, and clothes may be in disarray

If the individual has trouble with anxiety in addition to depression, the signs can be very different. They might be agitated which can show up as breathing rapidly, talking and walking faster than normal, or their arms might be crossed to protect their inner core. Appearances can therefore be deceiving!

The purpose of this section is not to try to figure out what someone else is feeling by reading their body language, but rather to use these distinctions to help you have more influence over the way you feel. The name of the game is to act the part you want to play, and use the *outward appearance* of contrasting emotional states for ideas to guide you. Making conscious changes to the way you carry yourself can actually alter your emotional state right now. Let's see how.

Suppose you find yourself feeling down in the dumps at a particular moment in time. Notice how you are presenting yourself to the world, and use a mirror if you have to. Check out your facial expression, eye contact, posture, breathing rate and depth, the tone of your voice, how you're holding your shoulders, whether your arms are crossed, and anything else you might notice in terms of how you might appear to others.

Once you have scanned your body, I invite you to try an experiment. Make some simple, easy changes, as if you're playing the part of someone like my friend Lisa who looks happy all the time. You don't have to walk around with a fake smile pasted on your face. That would make you feel phony! Just make some genuine, even subtle changes geared toward acting, dressing, and pretending *as if* you were feeling upbeat. In other words, do what children do when they play: pretend.

If your face is expressionless, form a pleasant, comfortable smile, even if no one else is around. If you're looking down at the floor, the place we tend to look when we're saying self-defeating things to ourselves, try looking up and outward. If your shoulders are slumped over, pull them back and stick out your chest. How about the rate and depth of your breathing? If you notice it's shallow and fast, take some slower, deeper breaths. Make appropriate adjustments to the volume and tone of your voice, the speed of your walk, and the position of your arms. Act like you're feeling content… even if you're not.

Do you wear clothes that make a statement about how you are feeling? Try wearing something that makes you feel good when you wear it. If you have hair on your head, put some effort into making yourself proud of it.

I can't guarantee that all or even any of these changes will effect how you feel, but what would it hurt to experiment a little? Try out some of these changes like you're trying on new clothes to see how much you like them. If you don't like how one outfit looks, you can always take it off and try on a new one! Making a few simple changes to the way you look and act can do wonders for how you see yourself. Why not give it a try?

Act the part you would like to play.

*"There are only two ways to live your life. One is as though nothing is a miracle. The other is as though everything is a miracle."*

ALBERT EINSTEIN

# TREAT YOUR BODY AS A MIRACLE

"There it is. There's the heartbeat!" In the darkened ultrasound room lies a woman whose seven-year quest in vain for a child is about to come to an end. Years of pain and sorrow at being unable to conceive will soon be replaced by unmitigated bliss, as the achievements of modern medicine have finally borne fruit in her life. The process of a new creation has finally begun.

My choice in careers as a specialist in fetal medicine has furnished me with a window into the magical flowering of new life. For the most part, regardless of race, ethnicity, religion, or culture, all unborn babies look exactly the same. I could look at "normal" ultrasounds as just another mundane part of my job that I do day after day; or I could recognize that peering through this window into creation every day places me on hallowed ground where I have the luxury of becoming a witness to life's blessings. Although sometimes I find myself engaging in the former, I much prefer the latter.

How easy it is to take our own bodies for granted, to treat them without respect to their rightful place in our lives as true gifts bestowed upon us by nature, as our own everyday miracle. Despite outward appearances that become coarser with age, we inherently know not to judge a book by its cover, as our brain, heart, and other essential organs act in concert to function like no man-made creation could ever do. If you're not sure about this, try building another *you* from scratch!

We know deep down in our hearts how amazing the inner workings of our bodies are, but we seem to forget time and time again that this is true. We take our bodies for granted, sometimes to the point of abuse. We eat too little or too much, choose the wrong foods, fail to get enough rest, and deprive this sacred vessel of adequate exercise and fun!

We make many valid excuses for our neglect. We're too tired, too busy, and too frustrated by past failed attempts at achieving tangible goals. We cave in to our emotional sufferings – loneliness, anxiety, sadness, frustration – that cause us to eat poorly, as we seek out the one pleasure we're always capable of having, but that eventually proves fleeting as it is soon replaced by regret. We put off getting that delightful massage whose healing energy we so enjoy, as we are "too busy" to take the time. We ultimately give up trying to deliver the nurturing care our bodies deserve, thus resigning ourselves to whatever fate has in store for us as a result of our own self-abuse and neglect.

The starting point for change is not another new diet, a new exercise regimen, or a new book to read. The place to start is with adopting a new attitude. To paraphrase German philosopher Friedrich Nietzsche, when it comes to revering your body, until you have a *why* you will never need a *how*. Once you have your *why*, the *how* will take care of itself, and you will be at peace with your body.

Send the same love and affection toward your body as you would send to your own child whom you adore. Treat it as a treasure that deserves to be protected. When it wants to dance, allow it to dance. When it grows weary and needs some rest, then give it just the right amount. At times it will crave comfort and you would be wise to heed this request. At other times it will cry out for healing and you will faithfully oblige. At every opportunity allow it to seek its own pleasures, and share in the joy of celebration with others. And when firm guidance is needed to bring your body back in line, take this responsibility seriously, as any conscientious parent would. Accept your body unconditionally as nature intended it to be, and you will be at peace with this part of you.

Love your body as you would adore your child, as the wonder that it is, and you need never ask for a better *why*. Listen for its quiet pangs to guide you toward just the right mix of Comfort, Healing, and Joy. In the long run it is not how *long* you live, but rather how *well* you live that truly matters.

Treat your body as a miracle.

*"'Tis not enough to help the feeble up, but to support them after."*

William Shakespeare

# Build Lasting Connections

Spring is an awesome season where I live. Early April rain summons in the cherry blossoms, which delight us for far too brief a time with their fragrant pink and white flowers whose departure heralds the onset of fresh green leaves. Summer is for shorts and T-shirts, barbeques, and watching children splash around in swimming pools. Fall is my favorite season, as it offers a welcome respite from the sweltering heat of summer. Warm sweaters are donned to take the bite out of crisp nighttime air, and Saturday football games seem to bring people together like nothing else can. Winter is a time for staying home to curl up with a good book under the watchful eye of a warm fire, a time for sharing hot chocolate and intimate conversation, and a time for quiet reflection on the year that has just passed.

Our personal lives also have their own seasons. We have our own unique cycles of birth and death, of health and disability, of intense joy and intolerable sorrow. I don't know about you, but I would hate to try to manage all these seasons alone. I know I am strong enough to cope with whatever comes my way in life, but I surely wouldn't want to have to go through it by myself, without the love and support of those who mean the most to me. Conversely, I consider it a privilege and a duty to help see others through their own unique challenges.

Whether one is going through a rough patch in life or not, having solid attachments to others is a vital component of emotional well-being. Humans are social beings, and most of us are not wired to be hermits living in a cave, or gurus spending days meditating in the mountains. Having healthy, nurturing relationships with others is one of the true joys of living.

When going through tough times, having strong connections with others is even more important than during smooth times. Having others we can depend on, and who can hopefully depend on us, helps give us strength to cope with those seasons in life when there is no fruit to harvest, and in some cases no seeds to plant for next year.

When winter is upon you, on whom do you depend? Perhaps old friends and new, family members, a romantic partner, clergy, co-workers, social networking buddies, a therapist, a social worker?

If you don't have enough people to talk to or support you, I suggest you begin to invite them into your life. Call an old friend and rekindle the connection, make new friends on the Internet, join a local club to meet others with shared interests, strike up a conversation with someone you see every day, or build bridges with others by volunteering to help a cause that is meaningful to you. You have to start somewhere!

If you currently have a strong web of support people in your life, be thankful, draw on it for support when you need it, and take the time to strengthen these bonds by offering others *your* support whenever you can, as you may be in a different season in your life than they are in theirs. Let them know that you are ready to serve them, that "I am here for you no matter what."

The bottom line is that having a strong support system is an integral part of living a healthy emotional life. Relying on others is a sign of strength, not weakness. Just as the whole is often greater than the sum of its parts, so too is a network of support stronger and more powerful than the sum of its individuals.

Being and feeling connected to others who support you, as you do your level best to navigate the myriad of life's challenges, is paramount to leading a healthy and fulfilling life. I hope you recognize this basic human need for forming emotional bonds with other people. I know I do.

Build lasting connections.

*"The first duty of love is to listen."*

PAUL TILLICH

# Listen With All Your Heart

Regardless of what season of our lives we are in, it is very easy to get totally preoccupied and self-absorbed about our current situation, especially during dark periods. At times, for many of us, we tend to obsess about our lives. We analyze and spend loads of time trying to "figure it all out" as we go about the futile search for answers to life's unanswerable questions. We try to think our way out of our emotional funk which only serves to make us feel worse.

One of the hardest things to do when you're down or merely just busy, is to listen to another human being. I'm not referring to "hearing" what they are saying, I mean genuine, uninterrupted, compassionate "listening." There are scores of books out there that instruct readers to develop the "skill" of listening, but that's not the kind of listening I am speaking about. The kind of listening I'm referring to requires no books to read, no instruction, and no practice. Anyone can do it, but few will. It is spiritual. It comes from the heart.

Have you ever had anyone in your life truly listen to you with all their heart?

I am not naturally skilled at everyday listening as I tend to multi-task too much. I often "man-listen," which means you can't count on me to remember what you just told me five minutes ago. At any given moment, I might find myself either preoccupied with my own thoughts, or thinking about what I want to say next when you are finished speaking, or feeling in too much of a hurry to concentrate.

But when I decide to put everything else down to listen, really listen with all my heart, the world... seems... to... stop. "You" become "thou" in my world, and I am totally engaged with you. This kind of listening is an act of love. It is a gift.

One of the best antidotes I know for reversing a negatively-charged emotional state is to give of myself to others. The trouble is that the last thing I may be thinking about when I am feeling this way is the act of giving of myself to another person. I just don't always feel like it! During these periods, it just doesn't make sense for me to focus on anyone other than myself. This is a big mistake!

When I am so preoccupied with "figuring it all out" on my behalf (me-focused), before I can consider being able to give to you (you-focused), nothing changes inside of me. I am no better off by all this *thinking!* Yet, when I make the decision to immerse myself in you, to merge my heart with yours, not only does it engage you, comfort you, and make you feel loved, it transforms *me* from the inside out. It is the proverbial win/win situation.

For just a few moments in time, however often you are able, and to whatever extent you can muster up the energy, give the gift of listening to someone who needs it. Merge your heart with theirs. Do it because their souls are so easily and profoundly nurtured by it, and because yours is too.

Listen with all your heart.

# Healing

*"All healing is first a healing of the heart."*

Carl Townsend

*"Men's thinking that you must halt before the barrier of inner negativity. You need not. You can crash through. . . whatever we see a negative state, that is where we can destroy it."*

MARQUIS DE VAUVENARQUES

# TEAR DOWN YOUR WALL!

For nearly 30 years, the Berlin Wall stood as a physical boundary between democratic West Berlin and communist-controlled East Germany. From the standpoint of free democracies such as the United States and most of Western Europe, the wall represented a symbolic barrier to freedom.

Then something wonderful happened.

In a 1987 speech given in Berlin, Germany, to commemorate the 750th anniversary of the city, President Ronald Reagan issued a challenge to Mikhail Gorbachev, General Secretary of the Communist Party of the Soviet Union. "... if you seek peace... Mr. Gorbachev, tear down this wall!" At the time, the notion of freedom for citizens of East Berlin seemed far-fetched and unrealistic. Maybe some day, yes, but not now. Yet against great odds, just two years later the wall started coming down with hammers and chisels wielded by people from all corners of the world. From coin-sized pieces to large slabs of crushed concrete, freedom and prosperity had arrived.

Within our minds, we can also have a wall — an *emotional* wall — comprised of negative thoughts and feelings that serve as a barrier to our freedom and prosperity, keeping us feeling "stuck" and unhealthy. Though this wall may not be visible to the naked eye, it nonetheless can keep us in bondage, separated from that which gives us joy on the other side. Our emotional wall can feel just as real as one made of concrete.

If you have a wall that acts as a barrier to your emotional freedom, please read on.

You can try to dig a tunnel underneath, climb over, or drill through it, but it remains in place. You try to overlook it, but it's hard to ignore living in a shadow when all you want is some sunlight. You could try to accept this wall as fate and give up trying to escape thereby resigning yourself to a life that's not nearly what you had hoped for, or... you can vow to do something about it!

If you want to experience true freedom from inner oppression, you have only one choice:

*Tear down your wall!*

If you are a "worry-wart," tearing down the wall may not seem so simple or even realistic. "That's just the way I am," you might say. If you find yourself often feeling anxious or gloomy, I wouldn't blame you for feeling skeptical about ever taking down barriers that seem insurmountable.

Tearing down the barriers to freedom is not always fun or easy. In fact, it can be downright hard work, a real pain in the you-know-what. The key to success in dismantling this wall is a willingness to try something new. That's all you really need. Because if you have the attitude that you are willing to put some elbow grease into this project and persistently chip away at it, your wall can come down one chunk at a time.

I hope you are somewhat skeptical about your ability to accomplish this task. A healthy dose of skepticism is a great way to protect yourself from disappointment. Just remember though, that you can remain skeptical on one hand, while keeping an open mind on the other. That's the attitude I hope you'll take with you as you embark on this endeavor.

If you are unwilling to consider the possibility that you could experience emotional freedom, then you're probably correct. The thought, "It'll never work" can serve as a self-fulfilling prophecy. As Henry Ford once said, "If you think you can do a thing or think you can't do a thing, you're right." Therefore, just the mere thought that something won't work can make it so.

We start with the basic premise that *thoughts* create *feelings*. Negative thoughts generate negative feelings, positive thoughts create positive feelings, and a combination of both types leads to feeling "mixed" or confused.

The truth is we all have negative thoughts that pop up automatically from time to time. Many of them are not even true, or are only partially true. Thoughts, in effect, can lie, exaggerate, or distort the truth. People who consider themselves "happy" see plenty of negative thoughts pass by them during the course of a day. If you're not sure, just find someone high up on the happiness scale and ask them. "Unhappy" people get plenty of negative thoughts, too, and they often don't mind sharing that fact with others. Of course, calling people *happy* versus *unhappy* is too simplistic, but I am using these terms to make the point that negative thoughts are not solely in the domain of certain kinds of people.

When our negative thoughts generate bothersome feelings they form an emotional barrier that separates us from our ability to feel "alive" and free. If we become preoccupied by our thoughts to the extent that we can't enjoy life, we feel stuck. Fortunately "stuck" really only means "stopped," because this state of mind is only temporary if you know what to do about it.

If everyone has negative thoughts, what then is the difference between those individuals who find a great deal of enjoyment in life and those who get stuck? The short answer is that several factors interact to determine well-being, among them our genetic make-up, our life circumstances, and, last but certainly not least, *how we react to our thoughts*. Our response to our thoughts is the one component of happiness that we can profoundly influence. Becoming a master at identifying our negative thoughts and reacting to them in a healthy way, rather than as a victim, can help us overcome any disadvantages we might have in terms of our genetic makeup or life circumstances.

Tearing down the wall so that you can taste freedom and experience joy does not require a sledgehammer or a chisel, but rather *a pen and some paper*. It probably won't happen overnight. It may take some time to eradicate that wall, as little by little, in large slabs and small, pieces of it simply crumble and blow away. Stubborn chunks might have to be made increasingly lighter through repeated effort before finally collapsing into a pile of dust. Getting rid of deeply hidden pieces requires first exposing and eliminating more superficial ones. But sooner or later, enough of the wall will start to come down that a ray of light will eventually shine through, and you will experience a newfound blow for freedom. The rest will quickly follow. It is only a matter of time.

Both positive and negative thoughts and images "appear" absolutely real to us, whether they actually represent the truth or not. That is why we are so apt to believe them without question. When we feel bad about something, we often cannot detect the thought that preceded that feeling. The thought or image can occur so quickly – even in an instant – that we assume the bad feeling appeared suddenly out of thin air.

While oftentimes we have no difficulty recognizing the negative thoughts and images that we carry around, sometimes they flash into our minds imperceptibly. I used to hear rumors about subliminal ads strategically placed within a movie whereby, for example, a hot dog flashes on the screen for a split-second outside the viewers' noticeable awareness, and people who didn't even know they were hungry suddenly find themselves getting up to go to the concession stand to buy a hot dog. Upsetting thoughts or images can flash through our minds just as quickly, leading us to react to them with an inexplicable *bad feeling* whose source is as elusive as that of the hot dog. In other words, we assume that the rotten feeling magically appeared out of thin air, when in reality it did not: a "single frame" of a thought or image created it all along.

The trick is to "catch" a potentially upsetting thought or image as soon as it pops up or shortly thereafter, before you get too caught up in the grip of the negative emotion that it produces. Once you're gripped by that emotion it's pretty tough to think straight, and you're stuck with having to wait out the painful state until the natural cycle of your moods washes it away.

Once you recognize it, you have two choices: You can let it pass on, like a dark cloud passing overhead, and be done with it, or you can "do something about it" if it begins to bother you or you're not sure if you can let it go easily. What you choose to do about it is where the interesting part begins. A virtually unlimited number of exercises and techniques are available to quell an unhealthy thought or image, making it powerless over you, even those that have made you feel miserable, helpless, and hopeless in the past. The closer to its infancy you stand up to it, the easier it will be to get rid of it.

I will demonstrate one technique that you can do in approximately 5 minutes. Keep in mind that one-time results can be complete, partial or nothing at all. Even if that particular thought is completely defused, another one could quickly take its place, as if obliterating one chunk of the wall exposes yet another that was previously hidden.

Suppose you feel insecure because you believe the thought, "I am unlovable!"

Okay. So, you have this thought, "I am unlovable." Recognizing the thought behind the feeling is the hard part. The easy part is figuring out what to do about the thought, one that you may or may not even believe to be true. I've heard lots of people say they recognized *intellectually* that the thought was a lie, but they still felt bad about it *as if* it were true. In other words, they couldn't convince themselves of the *lie* on a deep emotional level. This is where the power of writing it out comes in.

On a blank sheet of paper, write out a *completely honest* assessment of the thought that you wish to drain of its poison, and re-state it in a way that is healthy, self-accepting, and completely true. Please don't try to take a short-cut by telling yourself, "I don't need to write it out. I can do it all in my head." If it's truly bothering you, even a little, it's worth picking up a pen for a few short minutes!

Here is my own made-up sample for illustration purposes, but you must supply your own text.

Original thought: *"I am unlovable."*

Your rebuttal:

*"This is simply not true. Many people love me including family, friends, colleagues, and patients. There are also different degrees of love and different definitions. It's probably true that some people don't love me, or at least don't love certain aspects of my personality. That's fair. A few people may even dislike me altogether, but that is an inescapable part of life. No one is universally loved. I have enough love in my life, and just because someone is upset with me — and I might even be wrong about that! — doesn't mean that they don't love me. I am loveable, and I've got the track record to prove it."*

Once you have finished with this exercise in your own words, re-read it slowly, make any corrections or additions you deem appropriate, and feel free to destroy what you have written, since you can't recycle it anyway. One of three things will happen: 1) That particular thought will stop bothering you; 2) It will bother you less, or 3) this exercise won't help you at all. If the latter happens, congratulations, you are now one step closer to finding an exercise that *does* help you with this thought.

There is not a one-size-fits-all answer for neutralizing the potentially uncomfortable effects of self-sabotaging thoughts. Even if a particular exercise helps the first time, there is no guarantee it will help the second or the third. Therefore it is extremely valuable to load up on numerous options to have at your beck and call, so that if one thing doesn't work, you can easily try something else. Filling you up with choices is one of the chief foundations of this book, especially this section on Healing. The number of strategies for dealing with unwanted thoughts and feelings is virtually unlimited, as you can even utilize your vast creativity to make up your own.

If you are successful at eliminating one bothersome thought, and another takes its place, that is not a failure, it's actually a success. It means you have chipped away at some of your wall to reveal a deeper slab of concrete. Start the process anew for the next thought and the one after that if necessary. At times, hopefully rare, it might feel that there is an endless array of negative thoughts and pictures coming at you, to the point where you feel like you're playing the child's game, "Whack-A-Mole." That's where one mole is pounded into the ground and another pops up in a different place followed by yet another in a seemingly endless game. If you find yourself inundated like this, don't overdo it with the written exercises. Take a break from them and keep busy until you're up to trying something new. The Berlin Wall wasn't built in one day and it didn't come down in one day either.

Tear down your wall!

*"Defend me, God, from myself."*

# Disarm Your Inner Bully

"Tiny, old, scratched, a little banged up, and above all cheap!" This is how I would describe my very first car, a pre-owned, white Datsun B210, with 5-speed manual transmission and a hole in the floor of the front passenger seat big enough to see through to the passing road underneath. I loved that car!

I was in medical school at the time and I needed wheels — *anything* to get me back and forth from where I needed to go. I didn't pine for a newer, bigger, flashier, more expensive car. Sure I would have taken an upgrade if it were offered to me. Who wouldn't? And I was certainly not an ascetic who deprived himself of the finer things in life merely for the sake of some moral principle. No, I simply didn't have much money, and whatever I could get to meet my basic needs was just fine with me.

How funny that I learned to accept my pathetic car easier than I learned to accept my not-so-bad self. Unlike my Datsun, my expectations of myself were sometimes so high and unrealistic that feeling secure about who I was and what I had already accomplished in my short life was a concept I could not yet embrace. No matter how "good" I was at this or that, how generous, loving, or well-meaning my intentions, I still had trouble looking past my own little dents and scratches.

My perfectionist tendencies often translated to an anxiety fomented by the gap between my *real* and my *ideal* self. The bigger the gap, the greater the angst, and the more urgent the need to find emotional security outside of myself. For me, "outside" myself meant primarily trying to please others, as validation from them seemed to work like a wonder drug that made me feel complete. I considered myself one of the lucky ones, though, as some people who feel incomplete take emotional refuge in drugs, alcohol, and other addictions to fill the void and numb the pain.

When I was a young adult, I had the misguided belief that self-improvement, namely getting better and better at *things*, could overcome everything that was missing in my life. What I learned was that raising the bar for what I could do better often led to some degree of satisfaction and was often worth doing, but the hole within me remained. To put it another way, no matter how high the bar that I could scale, the gap between *who I was* and *who I wanted to be* would remain.

Living a fulfilling life does not require giving up the dream for a nicer car, one that is shinier and plusher, with a more powerful engine, leather seats, a high-tech sound system, and a floor without holes. Quite the contrary! Misty-eyed dreaming, shooting for the stars, and continuous self-improvement are all worthy and desirable components of a healthy life, but *in order to have a prayer of feeling secure about yourself,* you must first learn to accept yourself exactly as you are, wherever you are, *right now.* To be clear, self-improvement and self-acceptance are not mutually exclusive, not an either-or proposition. Aspire to make *both* of these concepts an important priority in your life.

It's one thing to suggest to someone that they accept themselves as they are — suggesting is the easy part. It's quite another thing to show them *how* to do it. *Understanding* without *implementing* is not only unhelpful, it can make you feel downright frustrated as it gives you one more reason to feel inferior while you lament, "Why can't I just accept myself? Other people seem to be able to do so, even ones who don't try to better themselves nearly as much as I do."

I used to think that self-improvement merely required Doing (something I was good at), whereas self-acceptance was simply a matter of Being (something passive that I either had or I didn't have). Boy was I wrong! Well, partly. Self-acceptance does entail a *certain* amount of contemplation and reflection. For some people the peace that accompanies genuine self-acceptance seems to come naturally, perhaps without any conscious effort or even realization of this gift on their part. However, for those of us who are a little more challenged in this department, there is hope. We can bring out the big guns: a pen and some paper, and get to work.

Before you try your hand at a powerful writing exercise, I'd like to revisit the word *but*. In the chapter "Can You Give Yourself Some Approval?" I give *but* a bad name. After all, this tiny but potent word has the power to poison everything that came before it, canceling out compliments, "I really liked the cake, *but*...", damaging self-esteem, "I know I just donated one of my healthy kidneys, *but*...", killing dreams, "I would like to start writing a book, *but*...," and a whole host of other harmful effects.

Just like sour lemons can be turned into sweet lemonade, *but* can be turned on its head to help you gain a sense of deep appreciation for yourself. One thing is required of you and this change might not be easy to implement. In order for this exercise to work, you will have to fess up to the *truth* about yourself *as you see it*. I don't just mean the slightly sugar-coated "truth"; I mean the ugly, unvarnished, brutally honest truth. Any attempt to resist or cover up the real deal as you know it to exist deep down inside yourself will render this exercise completely useless. The good news is that all that is required is your total honesty. You can do that if you really want to, right?

Don't worry. Your secrets are safe with *you*! No one will ever know what you have written if you tear the paper to shreds or burn it when you are finished. It won't be of any use to you in the future anyway, as the power of this exercise exists in the act of writing and not in the ink on the paper. If you want to reap the benefits of this approach in the future, you'll need to repeat it.

Before we begin, let me warn you about what *not* to do. Do not go overboard on the truth by taking a kernel of truth and making stuff up around it. We are looking for something more along the lines of a confession to yourself, for yourself, so that you can put unrealistic expectations of yourself behind you and move toward a fresh start. So, be honest, yes, but be fair and stick to the truth.

To illustrate the how-to for accepting yourself, let's say there is a part of you that feels guilty for over-eating. We'll call that part of you the Attacker, and the self-accepting part of you the Defender, but you can name them whatever you want. Let the games begin...

> *Attacker: You pig! You say you're going to start eating healthy with at least some degree of moderation, and there you go again, stuffing your fat face!*

> *Defender: You know what, you're absolutely right. I did overeat and I'm not happy about it either. **But** you also must admit that I've really cut down lately. One reckless binge does not make me a pig.*

> *Attacker: What are you talking about? You have done this time and time again for years. It's no wonder you're afraid to get on the scale. You are hopeless and worthless.*

> *Defender: You've got another great point; I hate getting on the scale. **But** I'd rather focus on my eating habits than my weight anyway. As far as having done this many times, I can't argue with that. I have had a problem in this area, and there's a chance I will do this again despite my best intentions. **But** I intend to continue making progress going forward. I might have another setback, **but** even if I do, it won't be the end of the world, as I can still appreciate myself for who I am as a person with all my wonderful qualities.*

Accepting yourself over a single act of overeating that dredges up feelings of guilt is one thing, but what happens when the Attacker cuts much deeper than that, focusing on some longstanding "truth" that really hits below the belt? As an example, let's pick the common condition of being overweight. Just remember, this technique can be modified to anything about yourself for which you feel you lack the appropriate amount of self-acceptance, even if it's something that you're trying to change. Remember also that you don't have to accept yourself completely; partial acceptance is better than none. However much self-acceptance you feel is appropriate at a given time is the amount that is just right for you.

*Attacker: You are so fat! How can you stand to look at yourself in the mirror? You should feel horrible about your appearance, so what are you smiling about?*

*Defender: It's true. I am overweight, and not just a little bit either, **but** I can stand to look at myself even though it does bother me at times. You are also correct that sometimes I do feel pretty darn frustrated about it, **but** I keep smiling because I have a life to live, and I refuse to allow my family trait of being overweight to get in my way if I can help it.*

*Attacker: Family trait? You act as though you bear no responsibility for your condition. You're enormous, and it's because you eat too much. You are weak!*

*Defender: Once again you've made a valid observation. I do overeat at times, **but** at other times I do the best I can to eat healthy foods. I learned long ago that no matter what I do short of starving myself, I have this tendency toward being overweight. I wish things were different, **but** they're not. I might always struggle with this, **but** I know I've put forth my best effort most of the time and that's something I am pleased about.*

This dialogue can last as long as it needs to so that the Defender has the last word. Notice how disarming it was for the Defender to admit their shortcomings and to actually take responsibility for them rather than make excuses, thus giving them credibility. At the same time, they made sure that the truth didn't get exaggerated. They concluded each round with a vigorous defense against their character being attacked, confining the attack to the *behavior* or the *condition* and not the *person*.

Here is an added twist: If you find yourself having difficulty standing up to the Attacker, approach your dialogue with an attitude of defiance and anger, as this is no time to be concerned about being polite. In other words, get mad! If you are not averse to "cussing like a sailor," infuse the conversation with a profanity-laced tirade, replete with name-calling, that reflects the fact that you are fed up with the criticism you have received from this part of you, and this last instance is like the proverbial straw that broke the camel's back. I will skip the example this time.

Disarm your inner bully.

*"Forgiveness is the fragrance that the violet sheds on the heel that has crushed it."*

Mark Twain

# GIVE YOURSELF THE EXTRAORDINARY GIFT OF FORGIVENESS

Who can forgive the murderer of their own child? One man did. Meet Azim Khamisa.

*In 1995, Azim's only son Tariq, a 20-year-old college student and part-time pizza delivery man, was gunned down in a robbery by 14-year-old eighth grader, Tony Hicks. Tony was a member of a gang that lured Tariq to a fake address to deliver pizzas. When Tariq refused to hand over the pizzas, Tony shot him dead.*

*Rather than seek revenge, rather than curl up and die, the distraught father went down the extraordinary path of forgiveness.*

*"There were victims at both ends of that gun," he told a friend shortly after the murder. He added, "The quality of the rest of my life would hinge on how I handled this tragedy."*

*He reached out to the grandfather of his son's murderer, Ples Felix, to help heal the pain of both men. Azim established the Tariq Khamisa Foundation to teach kids alternatives to violence, and invited Ples Felix to serve in the foundation.*

I hope never to be called to emulate the divine achievement of forgiveness the way Azim Khamisa did in response to the senseless, unthinkable crime committed against his young son, and ultimately to himself. The truth is I am not sure that I could succeed. Yet, no one can be absolutely certain of their own capacity to rise above such a crushing blow until they actually come face to face with the heavy burden of preserving a life that is worth living – their own.

Fortunately most of us are not regular victims of this type of hurt inflicted by another human being. When we do feel like the innocent casualty of the callous behavior of others, we find ourselves challenged spiritually, emotionally, and psychologically, in ways for which we may not be prepared to respond. In short, how can we forgive? Perhaps even more relevant to the matter at hand: Why should we forgive? As I will soon hope to convince you, the *why* is the seed that yields the fruit of the *how*.

Forgive?

Who can forgive the drunk driver who maims or kills a loved one? Who can forgive the thief who pillages an unsuspecting elderly couple whose dreams of "golden" years vanish overnight? Who can forgive the perpetrator of sexual abuse, incest, rape, physical torture, or another horrendous crime that has wreaked havoc on the life of the powerless? One need not travel to the remains of Auschwitz to find ample evidence of man's inhumanity against his fellow man.

Maybe you haven't been injured to the tune of catastrophic proportions, but I can guarantee that you have suffered real pain, physical or emotional, at the hands of another. Who can forgive the hurt of a broken promise by a once-loving partner? Who can forgive the vindictiveness of a co-worker who sabotages a career out of spite? Who can forgive the stinging criticism of a loved one who is supposed to be in your corner?

Many people say they can't forgive; do not argue with them, for they are correct.

Lack of forgiveness ranges widely from simply holding a grudge over a perceived "slight" to harboring intense feelings of anger and resentment over an "unforgiveable" act. The victim of the injustice may believe that they are entitled to their anger, and that could very well be true. A victim has a right to be angry!

Before I characterize what forgiveness is, allow me to impart my view of what forgiveness is *not*. Forgiveness is not condoning the insensitive or heinous act of others. It doesn't excuse the boorish behavior of a colleague, the betrayal of a spouse, or the mouth that spews venom with disregard for its target. Forgiveness does not absolve the pedophile or spring the vandal.

Forgiveness is a remarkable gift that comes from inside of you; a gift not for them, but for *you!* Only for you. You don't forgive so that they'll feel better; you forgive so that *you'll* feel better as an act of self-interest rather than charity. You do it in order to move on with your life, not so that you can let the other person off the hook.

What happens when you hold on to resentment?

*"Resentment is like taking poison and waiting for the other person to die."*

Malachy McCourt

You now have the *why*.

Forgiving is a process, but true forgiveness is a destination; an "all-or-nothing" proposition. Make up your mind that you are going to forgive completely and permanently. Do not resign yourself to doing it because it makes you a good person — "I *should* do it because I *have* to" — do it because you know that you *must* in order to find peace.

You can find your peace all at once or a little bit at a time. You don't *try* to forgive — you just forgive. You need not forget in order to forgive either, as remembering the pain is not the same as owning it. Thus, let go of the pain, but feel free to keep the memory of it, as past lessons may serve as your mentor on some other day.

Now you need the *how* of forgiveness.

Ask yourself, as many times as necessary, "What would my life be like right now if I could forgive this transgression?" Listen for an answer. Don't try to force one to appear.

If you hear back, "I just can't," that isn't a problem. Simply say, "I know that I can't, but what would it be like if I *could*?" Use this question over and over again, changing it more to your liking if necessary, to activate your imagination to search within yourself for the possibility of forgiveness. You are looking only for the possibility, even one that is faint at first. Forgiveness cannot occur without first existing in your imagination as a possibility.

"But what if I *could*?"

Each time you hear your own retort, "But what if I could?" you draw one step closer to reaching your destination than you otherwise would have been. Any hope for forgiveness must first form in the mind — *your* mind — where through repeated inquiry, true forgiveness can begin to take shape. That is the only way I know how.

Give yourself the extraordinary gift of forgiveness.

*"Life does not have to be perfect to be wonderful."*

# Be Happy Now

Okay. I admit it. Telling someone to "Be happy now," especially when they might be going through tough times, seems pretty silly. Stay with me though, as there is a method to my madness. This book is all about the journey, not the destination.

Think back to any event – happy or sad – that occurred in your life exactly one year ago.

Hold this memory in your mind for just a few seconds. If I asked you to point with your finger toward that event from one year ago, where in the space around you would you direct your attention to point to that moment in time? Some people find that one year ago is located *behind* them; others will point to their *left* or in front of them. Where is "one year ago" located in your mind? Make a mental note of this location.

Next, picture yourself at any event that you anticipate will take place next year such as a birthday or holiday. Where would you point your finger when mentally imaging this future event?

We all store time in a way that is unique to us, along an imaginary timeline that exists outside our bodies. Many people keep their timeline in front of their bodies where they can "see" it, with the past on their left and the future on their right. For others the timeline passes right through their bodies starting from behind their back (past), and passing forward to the space in front of them (future). Imaginary timelines can be mentally placed in an infinite number of configurations and serve as places we use to store information, that is, images we remember from the past or imagine taking place in the future.

A common refrain that I have often heard people say begins with, "I'll be happy when..."

"I'll be happy when... I have more money."
"I'll be when... this relationship is fixed."
"I'll be happy when... I find the time to relax and have some fun."

A close cousin to this phrase is, "I won't be happy until..."

"I won't be happy until... I'm out of debt."
"I won't be happy until... I can quit this job."

If you ever utter these words to yourself, remember this: Whatever you use in your life to fill in these blanks has the same end result: You assume that you are currently lacking something, you are incomplete, and you will become whole again only after something in your life changes in the future. The trouble is that tomorrow never comes, *now* is put off yet another day, and you can never feel satisfied because even if circumstances do change to complete your life, there will always be items on your "To do" list that cause you to mentally postpone completeness until some time in the future. In other words, you have placed your fulfillment in a space outside of yourself, onto your future timeline where you can't reach it.

Why can't you reach it? Because happiness can never be enjoyed in the future, only in the "here and now."

I am not saying that every time someone says, "I'll be happy when…" that they are currently unhappy or not feeling fulfilled by other parts of their life. In fact, some individuals successfully motivate themselves using an intense desire to achieve what they do not currently have. Moreover, this sort of utterance is clearly used as an innocent figure of speech in many, if not most, cases. Therefore, not every casual comment along these lines warrants thoughtful introspection and analysis. But when this form of statement is pervasive enough that virtually "nothing" makes a person happy, or intense enough to upset the soul, self-correction is in order.

If this applies to you, the first thing to recognize is that the thought itself – "I'll be happy when…" – *is* the problem, not the piece that is missing in your life. To put it another way, the feeling of incompleteness is not caused by *what you don't have*. It's caused by the *thought* that you don't have it, thus creating within you the nagging, frustrating feeling of "lack." The process of placing your happiness outside of yourself onto your future timeline is simply a bad habit. If you were to suddenly achieve all your wants and desires, but spent tomorrow lamenting the absence of a whole slew of new ones, you would be back in the same boat, the feeling of incomplete and unsatisfied. The void inside of you would quickly re-emerge.

If this is true, then what can you do about it?

How do you enjoy the here and now *inside* of yourself rather than perpetually seeing contentment *outside* of you, in your future, where you can never quite reach it, conjuring up to some the familiar refrain of Shakespeare's Macbeth as he lamented, "Tomorrow, and tomorrow, and tomorrow"?

The answer lies in cultivating an attitude of *indifference to the outcome.* This is easier said than done. Having desires, goals, and aspirations is worthwhile. Planning for the future, and looking forward to it, is an integral part of emotional well-being. Just as an architect sketches a blueprint before a house is built, we must first create what we desire within our minds before we can create it outside ourselves. Trouble arises when we become too attached, too emotionally dependant on the outcomes we seek to manifest. When we *crave* rather than *allow*, we become preoccupied with what "isn't" present in our lives rather than what is possible. The more intensively we crave, the more painfully we suffer the emptiness of *not having*.

How do you plan for the future – a worthwhile and healthy endeavor – yet live for the Now, the only place where you can truly find joy? How do you stop clinging to the outcome you desire to alleviate the suffering that comes from wanting what you don't have?

As is often the case, the answer lies in the power of words you use to activate your imagination.

When you turn your assortment of demands over to your imagination, you unleash a mysterious life force that drives the promise of fulfillment from "over there" to the only place that offers the hope of finding it – back home within yourself, within the present moment. You start by planting seeds and trusting nature to decide what happens next. Nature might not give us everything we want, but at least we can do our part by supplying the fertile soil that may allow our hopes and dreams to flourish. There are no guarantees!

(1) When you catch yourself feeling the unease and discomfort that accompanies, "I'll be happy when…" or "I won't be happy until…" or some other variation of the same theme, first write down that thought.

*"I won't be happy until I have more money."*

(2) Change this statement of "lacking" into a statement of "having."

*"I open myself up to the abundance of the universe."*

Notice that we have performed a major makeover on the original bleak statement. We eliminated the negative "won't." Always state what you *do* want rather than what you *don't*.

We switched the specific term "money" into the more flexible one, "abundance," which is what we truly have in mind, as money is only one form of abundance. This keeps all options open rather than limiting them to one choice.

We also eliminated "until" — a future-oriented wish — in favor of "open myself up" — a present-oriented reality.

Here are some additional examples:

*"I will be happy when I stop feeling anxious in large crowds"* can become *"I welcome the possibility of relaxing in front of others."*

*"I won't be happy until I have paid off all my debts"* can become *"I allow myself to stay calm as I re-pay my obligations."*

Be creative. Play with the words and phrases to find those that resonate with you the most. Come up with new ways of expression that take away that empty feeling and replace it with an *openness to allow the possible* — a delightful sense of freedom and hopefulness that you can experience right now in this moment. It is as if you are opening your outstretched arms and embracing the universe with the attitude, "Here I am. I am open to you. These are my requests but use me as you wish as I am ready to receive whatever comes my way."

For those special situations in which the craving is intense, creating a powerful grip that keeps you feeling "stuck," there is a deeper way to reap the benefits of creatively articulating your words. Try writing a single paragraph that conveys your personal spirited defense against the powerful attachment which preoccupies your mind. Please formulate your own expression, as copying mine verbatim will do you no good. Here's one of an infinite number of ways to go about this exercise.

Old thought:

 "I can't be happy until I figure things out."

New thought:

"Nonsense. I have felt happy many times in the past when I didn't have everything figured out. In fact, no one can have all the answers they want at all times. That is just not realistic. While it is true I would strongly prefer to have some answers, not all questions are answerable, and even the ones that are might take some time and patience to unravel. Even if some of my questions are never, ever answered, I can live with that, as I have fully accepted major uncertainty many other times in my life. For now, *I am grateful for the clarity I do have and remain open and hopeful for more.*"

When you are finished, re-read what you wrote, fully absorbing its meaning. Make sure you are completely satisfied with the truthfulness of your new thought. You must believe everything you wrote wholeheartedly. After you are finished, feel free to shred it, as it has no further use to you. Then go about your day allowing your mind to be at ease. You can relax because any changes that may occur from this exercise will happen automatically without any further effort from you.

Be happy now.

*"There's no secret to balance. You just have to feel the waves."*

# See Your Choices With Clear Eyes – Make Your Choices With a Clear Conscience

Do you like candy? Perhaps you enjoy chocolate, or maybe you prefer some other kind of special treat. It doesn't really matter what your choice is, just pick something you love to eat.

Now suppose I am your best friend and just happen to have some of this delectable creation in my hand, and I break it in two for us – you and me – to share. Oops! One piece is bigger than the other. Now I've got both pieces in my outstretched hand, waiting for you to take one of them. Which one will you choose – the Little Piece or the Big Piece?

Each and every day you make the fundamental decision, sometimes dozens of times in a single day: Do you take the Little Piece or the Big Piece? Which one do you *really* want?

Allow me to explain.

The Little Piece signifies all those things in life that your conscience tells you that you *should* do. It symbolizes responsibilities. And believe me, if your life is anything like mine, you've got plenty of them! You go to work, take out the trash, care for others who rely on you, visit a sick friend, attend a funeral – the list goes on and on.

On the other side of my hand is the Big Piece. It represents those things that you *really want* to have, be, and do. It embodies freedom. This is where you have the most fun, indulge, relax, blow off steam, and otherwise enjoy yourself. When you go for a leisurely walk, take in a movie, get a bite to eat with friends, have sex (because you want to!), or generally unwind after a long day, you are taking the Big Piece. The list of possibilities is limitless, and fortunately most of our decisions about which piece to choose – the Big Piece or the Little Piece – do not, individually, entail major risk to our well-being.

*Do you sleep late or get up early to exercise?*

*Do you order the fresh fruit or the French fries?*

*Do you take the last serving of ice cream or leave it for someone else?*

Going back to my original question, which piece would you take?

I suspect if you're like most people and a friend gave you this choice, you'd probably pick the Little Piece, right? Many factors could play into your decision, both obvious and not-so-obvious ones, and chances are you won't spend too much time analyzing such a trivial choice. Maybe you'll take the Little Piece because you don't want your friend to think you're selfish, or perhaps taking the Big Piece would cause you to feel guilty. It could be that it just makes you feel good to give up the Big Piece, since doing so exemplifies restraint, or simply because you're on a diet!

On the contrary, just maybe you'll take the Big Piece because you took the Little Piece the last several times you had to choose with this friend, and you now feel that it's "my turn to get what I want." Or your *friend* is on a diet, and you want to do them a favor by sparing them the extra calories contained in the Big Piece.

Whichever decision you make at any given time doesn't necessarily matter much in the grand scheme of your life. The point is that these decisions represent your values, and in choosing your values you have some important say over how you feel in the long run. If you recognize that you are taking the Little Piece, you can either feel good about it or you can feel frustrated instead because you *really* wanted the Big Piece.

People get into trouble when they don't have balance in their lives between the choosing of the Little Piece or the Big Piece.

If you nearly always seem to take the Little Piece, your life will be filled with work and sacrifice and you may feel like a martyr. Your life is all work and no play. Have you had any fun, that is, have you taken the Big Piece lately?

If, however, like a child, you nearly always take the Big Piece, and your life is all about, "Me, me, me"– how are you likely to feel? Guilty! And feeling guilty about excessively taking the Big Piece doesn't exactly lend itself to enjoyment.

The trick is to have balance. Don't strive for fifty-fifty division between the two choices in order to achieve perfect alternation between them, but rather strive for some irregular mixture that over time allows you to fulfill your responsibilities *and* gives you permission to have fun! When you have the right mix *for you*, you will optimize your ability to pat yourself on the back for choosing the Little Piece and feeling entitled to indulge in taking the Big Piece. A healthy dose of both choices is vital for emotional and spiritual well-being.

The decision between the Little Piece and Big Piece does not necessarily have to be an either/or decision; in special situations it can be both. True magic occurs when the Little and Big Pieces converge; when we find joy in our work, when we feel wonderful about our sacrifices for others, and especially when we can't distinguish between the two choices because they are one and the same. These precious times when we find no distinction between the two pieces constitute a sacred gift to cherish as long as it lasts.

When the choice isn't clear and much is at stake, what should you do? The best action to take is to *wait*. Hope-filled waiting combined with a readiness to receive an answer sends an invitation to a brilliant part of you deep down that knows instinctively what to do. Wait for your inner wisdom, your intuition, to guide you in the right direction. Be prepared to receive this message by opening yourself up to listening for the gentle whisper of the wise inner voice that signals the right course of action, a voice that speaks to you when you least expect it, day or night. To put it simply: let your conscience be your guide.

See your choices with clear eyes - make your choices with a clear conscience.

*"Let us be silent, that we may hear the whispers of the gods."*

RALPH WALDO EMERSON

# LISTEN FOR THE SOUND OF THE CALL TO ACTION

Do you enjoy going to the movies? How about cuddling up with a good novel, delighting in a play, or relishing in the beauty of a musical production? No matter what form of entertainment you're drawn to, each tells a story of some sort, a story about life.

In the telling of virtually all stories in various formats, the Hero of the story starts out living in the world of familiarity, only to become challenged to "rise to the occasion" by forces from within or without. In the celebrated musical, *The Wizard of Oz*, for example, Dorothy is compelled to react to circumstances that have befallen her:

*Having claimed Toto trespassed into her garden, chased her cat, and bit her, Miss Gulch arrives with a court order from the sheriff to take Toto, and rides away with him on her bicycle. When Toto escapes and returns to Dorothy, Dorothy decides at that moment they must both run away from home.*

Our own lives may not be as dramatic or predictable as in fictional accounts, but we are nonetheless the hero in our own personal journeys through life, a hero who is often called upon to stand up to challenges that we neither ask for nor desire. Whether we face up to our trials at all and how vigorously and effectively we respond requires, of course, that we hear the Call to Action in the first place.

Examples of such Calls to Action may include:

- My marriage is in trouble.
- My body is not healthy.
- I'm feeling "down" a lot these days.
- I often get anxious.
- My finances are coming apart.
- I'm unhappy at work.
- I'm having trouble dealing with anger.
- I've got an unhealthy addiction to the Internet or something else.
- I've been hit by an illness, accident, or act of nature.
- I can't sleep!

The list of possibilities is endless.

We stand the greatest chance of hearing our Calls to Action when we create the conditions for them to be heard. That means setting some time aside to turn down the noise that we often use as a distraction to attempt to drown out the sounds. Some people use food, alcohol and other drugs, television, the Internet, cell phones, and even exercise to keep themselves from hearing the approaching drumbeat of the Call to Action. When we turn off these distractions from time to time, we give our inner wise voice – our intuition – a fighting chance to be heard, telling us where we need to focus our attention the most.

Spend time in quiet solitude. Give yourself time and space for inner reflection. Take walks in the park. Contemplate the miracles that surround you. Meditate regularly. Lie awake in bed for an extra few minutes in the morning to be able to hear your inner voice.

Even when we do hear a Call to Action, we often reject dealing with it outright or we attempt to postpone it, as in, "Out of sight, out of mind." We don't want to open up a new can of worms since we have enough on our plate already. It could be that we are the sort of person who only responds to problems when they reach crisis proportions. We are too busy, too stressed, and out of time.

Calls for Action do not all share the same degree of urgency. Obstetricians like me encounter Calls to Action as an integral part of the job when it comes to planning a Cesarean delivery, commonly referred to as a C-section. Though the end-result is the same — delivery of a baby through surgery — the element of timeliness is not. These surgeries can be divided into three types: Stat, Urgent, and Scheduled.

Stat C-sections must happen *right now*. Nurses wheel the patient rapidly down the hall to the operating room, the anesthesiologist puts her to sleep, and the doctors quickly scrub their hands. This is no time for small talk, and our only focus is to *get the baby out now!* "Stat" represents *crisis*.

Urgent C-sections take place quickly, but the staff can take their time. The fetal heart rate tracing shows signs of possible stress, but not distress, and the luxury of time that the absence of crisis affords allows for careful preparation for the procedure. "Urgent" means that time is running out, but enough time exists for safety, focus, and precision.

Scheduled C-sections are planned procedures that simply accommodate the schedule of the surgeon and patient. Most commonly these are performed because the woman had a C-section in the past and either cannot or will not try for a vaginal delivery. Thus, she schedules her surgery around the time the baby is due. When surgery is scheduled, the atmosphere is *relaxed*.

When you are presented with a Call to Action and are being asked by life to rise to the occasion, at what stage do you typically respond? Do you act early, taking steps to head problems off at the pass, or do you allow them to grow and fester, risking the culmination of a crisis?

No matter what stage you find yourself responding to, the only way you'll even have a chance to act early is if you hear the Call to Action in the first place. Only then can you decide *whether* and *how decisively* you plan to act.

Listen for the sound of the Call to Action.

*"You can tell whether a man is clever by his answers. You can tell whether a man is wise by his questions."*

NAGUIB MAHFOUZ

# Stop Asking the Wrong Questions... and Ask the Right Ones!

"Why do I feel so bad?"

"How come life is so unfair?"

"What are they trying to do to me?"

"When is it going to be my turn?"

"Where are all the decent people?"

These questions, and an infinite number like them, are questions we have all probably asked ourselves from time to time. In some strange way we derive a certain comfort from feeling like a victim of life's circumstances, and I am no exception.

The trouble is that these questions are disempowering. They assume that things are bad and have no easy answers. This anguished grieving over life's circumstances fosters a sense of hopelessness and helplessness. In terms of enhancing our lives, these questions not only serve no good purpose; they actually make us feel worse about our existence than we already did.

When you find yourself feeling bad for no obvious reason, check to see whether you're asking yourself some sort of disempowering question. If you can't find one on the surface, dig deeper to see whether you're "presupposing" a question such as, "Why does my life suck so much?"

The mere act of recognizing a disempowering question shines a spotlight on it and exposes it for what it is: a self-defeating thought. Once this happens, can you think of an alternative, more empowering question, one that induces your creative imagination to search for solutions to your challenges, rather than obsess about "What's missing" from the picture of your ideal life?

"Why do I feel so bad?" becomes "What can I do to feel better?"

"How come life is so unfair?" becomes "How can I enhance my well-being?"

"What are they trying to do to me?" becomes "How can I communicate my feelings to those who seem to be expressing ill will toward me?"

"When is it going to be my turn?" becomes "What could I do to improve my choice of opportunities?"

"Where are all the decent people?" becomes "Where shall I look to find friends who are supportive of me?"

It's okay to complain about life sometimes by asking unanswerable questions. It is true that sometimes life *can* be unfair, unkind, upsetting, and painful. Feel free to look at a little bit of complaining as a part-time indulgence that can be "fun" to share with friends in a "bitch" session. But when the complaining doesn't just reflect what you're bummed out about and actually *contributes* to it, it is time to take a serious look at re-phrasing your questions. Wise questions beget wise answers.

Stop asking the wrong questions... and ask the right ones!

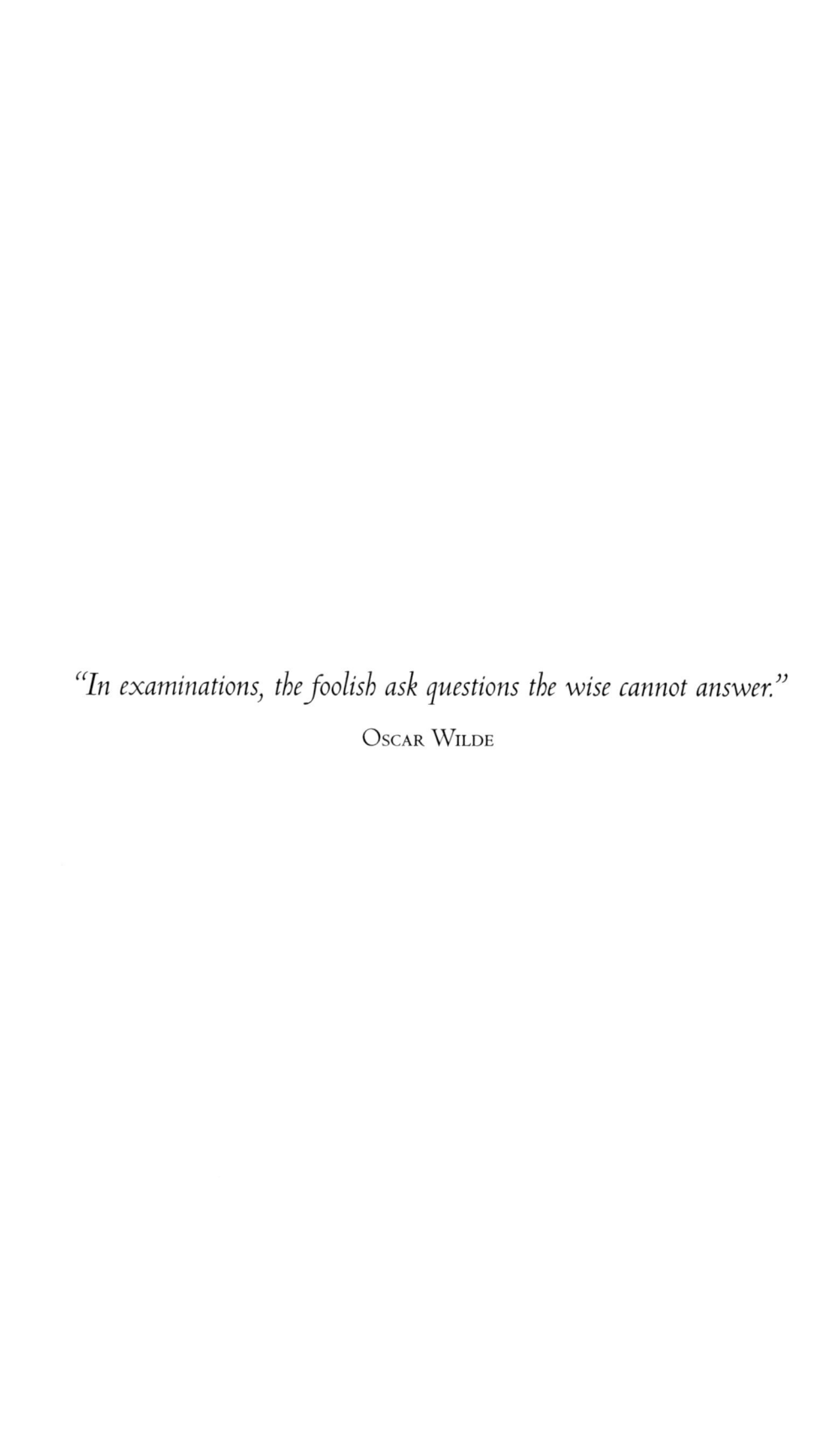

*"In examinations, the foolish ask questions the wise cannot answer."*

Oscar Wilde

# BEWARE OF "WHY"

When I was a kid, one of my favorite TV shows was "Lost in Space," a modern-day version of Robinson Crusoe that portrayed the adventures of a family marooned in outer space on a succession of planets. The most distinctive part of the show for me was when the Robot with the human voice waved his mechanical arms and bellowed out, "Danger, Danger!" in an effort to protect the family from harm's way.

When I hear someone who is in a bad mood start asking questions that begin with the word "why," an alarm goes off within me that cries out, "Danger, Danger!" Some prime examples of "Why" questions are:

Why does this always happen to me?
Why doesn't anything ever go my way?
Why are people so mean?
Why can't life be easier?

While in some cases asking "why" can be useful, many times it is not as it can actually make matters worse. We might think we ask "why" *because* we feel bad, and that might in fact be true initially. But asking "why" can also *cause* you to feel bad, as it perpetuates a never-ending cycle of doom and gloom.

Our minds have a way of answering the questions we feed them. The trouble is we are often not consciously aware of the questions we are asking ourselves. Rest assured, our mind *will* come up with an answer, just not always the kind of answer that is, emotionally-speaking, good for us. The upsetting emotions that result can then propagate even more asking of the question "why," causing such feelings to spin around inside of us with ever-increasing momentum, ultimately taking on a life of their own.

If you ask, "Why does my life seem so rotten?" your mind will happily oblige you with an answer by engaging your memory to find examples of painful periods when your life really did feel rotten, never mind the joyful times that intervened. How will this make you feel? Terrible.

When you ask, "How many more things can go wrong?" you will engage your imagination to create a whole slew of mental pictures showing in luminous detail what could go wrong, and in how many possibilities the scenario could play out.

The next time you feel bad about something and you notice the word "why" rolling around in your head, think "Danger, Danger!" Write out the entire "why" question on a piece of paper if you find it troublesome, so that you can take a good, hard look at it. This gives you a handle on the problem.

What then?

The way to interrupt the self-defeating nature of "why" is to re-formulate the question by asking "what, how, or when" instead, which immediately allows you to switch from playing emotional defense to offense, a transformation that holds the promise of arriving at a satisfying and peaceful state of your mind.

"Why is this happening?" can be converted to:

What am I going to do about it?
How can I solve this?
When is the best time to start?

These are the questions you should be asking yourself.

Beware of "why."

*"The essence of being human is that one does not seek perfection."*

GEORGE ORWELL

# Choose the Path of Excellence Over the Myth of Perfection

A fine line exists between the beauty of what can be and the agony of what will never be. Choosing which side of the line to live on means the difference between one who embraces a challenge versus one who fends off frustration; between one who accepts and one who blames; one who forgives and one who rejects.

Which side of the line would you rather live on?

You can tell which side of the line you are on by the words that you use. "Should," "must," "ought," and their negative forms, all belong on one side. They variously refer to what you did or did not do in the past and what you feel powerfully obligated to do in the future. They reflect an inexhaustible set of rules, and they show no mercy.

"I should exercise more."
"I should have eaten less."
"I should never feel anxious."

"I should..., I should..., I should..."

We also use "shoulds" to control the behavior of others, to lay guilt trips on them and make ourselves feel morally superior. We direct this type of behavior at our children, our partners, relatives, strangers, even our friends. And even when we're not saying it out loud to them, we're thinking it to ourselves.

"You should…, You should…, You should…"

In our efforts to be morally upright people, too often we set up an ideal of moral perfection that leads to the unhealthy habit of beating ourselves up for things we have or haven't done, or feeling the immense pressure of doing or not doing things we have yet to face. The resulting feelings of guilt, frustration, and anxiety can take on a life of their own, lowering our sense of self-esteem and negating both the pleasure of what we have accomplished and the promise of what we haven't.

Don't get me wrong. We do have responsibilities to ourselves and others that constitute "shoulds" and "should nots" in a literal sense. Parents "should" take care of their dependant children. Friends "should" listen; teachers "should" teach; society "should" help the elderly and infirm; the world "should" reject genocide.

But from the standpoint of being at peace with ourselves, and with other people for that matter, there is a vital distinction that defines the two sides of the line: one that demarcates moral achievement on one hand, and moral failure on the other. The side we live on reflects whether we view the sweetness of life as being derived from the journey itself, replete with all its ups and downs, or from some sort of mythical destination that always remains beyond our reach with each step that we take.

What this all boils down to is the difference between striving for *perfection* – a fantasy world that can only be visited through spirited imagination – and striving for *excellence* – an attitude of continuous, ongoing, realistic endeavors that can be yours at any time. The beautiful alternative to perfection therefore, is not mediocrity, it is excellence!

The roots of perfection-striving are ostensibly fed by the desire for love and acceptance, yet quite the contrary is true if you think about it. Who would you rather spend your time around: someone who is "perfect" all the time or someone who revels in their own unique set of little flaws?

I'm not suggesting you totally eliminate words like "should" from your vocabulary as that would be unrealistic and unnecessary. What I *am* suggesting is that when you find yourself feeling bad because of unmet expectations of yourself or others, and you can decipher an implicit "should" in your thinking, this is a call to action to put an end to the misguided hunt for perfection.

How is this done?

It's easy in theory to make the philosophical case to strive for excellence rather than perfection. After all, virtually everyone knows that perfection is not attainable — "I know I *shouldn't* say 'should'" — but what practical tools are available to end the feelings of failure and perverse judgments and restore you to a healthy sense of wholeness?

One powerful way to interrupt the "should" cycle is to replace *should, ought, need,* and *must* as well as their negatives, with what I call soft words, namely words that heal. Healing words include: *lovely, beautiful, delightful, wonderful, sweet, refreshing, amazing, great, nice, terrific,* and *fantastic.* Not only can you replace "should" words with kinder, gentler words, you can also pose the statements as questions.

Instead of saying, "I should exercise more often," how different would you feel if you said, "Wouldn't it be *lovely* if I exercised more often?"

"I shouldn't have eaten so much," becomes "It would have been *great* if I had eaten a smaller portion."

"I should never get upset," is nicer as "Wouldn't it be *wonderful* if I learned to accept all my emotions?"

"I should have called more often," is better expressed as "It would have been *nice* had I taken the time to call."

Hopefully you agree that the latter sounds are easier on the ears and their vibrations are softer on the heart, as they are less incriminating and thereby less threatening to your self-esteem. That's the point. These words are not designed to excuse you from bona fide personal responsibilities and assuage your guilt so that you can feel free to shirk them. They are intended to do the opposite; that is keep you merrily on the path of excellence rather than the doomed path to an imaginary perfection that exists only in your mind.

Choose the path of excellence over the myth of perfection.

*"Always and never are two words you should always remember never to use."*

WENDELL JOHNSON

# Two Words You Should Always Remember Never to Use

One of the happiest days of my life was the day I got my driver's license. To a 16-year-old boy, a driver's license means freedom. Of course, I first had to learn to drive and that took a little time. Before anyone can learn to drive, they have to learn the basic rules of how a car works.

After learning how to start the car and steer it, the next step is to find out what those pedals on the floor do. The first car I learned to drive had an automatic transmission with two pedals. I learned that the one on the right was the gas and the one on the left controlled the brakes. The second car I sat in had a manual transmission with three pedals. Once again, the pedal on the right was the gas pedal. In the third car I ever drove as well as the fourth, the pedal on the right was the gas pedal. Priding myself on being a quick learner, I came to conclude that that pedal on the right is *always* for the gas, and the pedal on the left is *never* in charge of that particular function.

Similarly, as a young child I learned that the thing called a "door knob" opened not only the doors in my house, but the ones in everyone else's house, too. Same thing goes for the button that turns on a computer and the handle that flushes a toilet. We all have the capability to generalize countless everyday experiences to make our lives predictable. In most situations this is a very good thing, as it makes the world easier to navigate.

When it comes to our relationships with ourselves and others, this ability to generalize can have its drawbacks.

When someone trips, we say, "He fell." The second time he falls we say, "Look, there he goes again." The third time, "He *always* falls." The fourth time we put a label on him: "He is a klutz!"

Some people are programmed to do this with themselves ("I always screw up. I am such an idiot!"), and with their children ("You flunked another test. You'll never amount to anything!"). Accepting this kind of criticism as fact is the essence of low self-esteem. It can be automatic such that people don't even realize that they're doing this, and it's very, very harmful. In fact, when a person "sees" themselves as being a "loser" or a "failure," this self-perception can become a self-fulfilling prophecy, and actually *cause* them to lose or fail, which just reinforces what they have been telling themselves all along. It becomes a vicious cycle.

The language that we use, both inside our heads as thoughts and through our lips as words, speaks volumes about how we interpret information. Saying, "I failed" might be a valid description of what happened. Saying, "I always fail" is very different and simply wrong! No one always fails. Going one step further to "I am a failure," it becomes no longer a description: it is a judgment, an untrue label that is harmful to one's emotional well-being. While it is true that a person can fail at a given endeavor, no one *is* a failure in their totality.

The answer to these harmful lies we tell about ourselves and others is to stop telling them! It sounds simple — and it is — but it is very possible. The trick, as is often the case, is first to be aware that you are thinking and speaking those potentially damaging words *always* and *never* about yourself and others. Once you realize this, just replace these words with *sometimes* or *often*.

The emotional impact of saying, "I always screw things up" can be dampened when it's changed to, "I sometimes screw things up." If you want to lessen the emotional impact even further, "I sometimes screw things up" can be transformed into, "I sometimes make an honest mistake."

Since *always* and *never* usually culminate in name-calling, you can take the sting out of that behavior, too. The declaration that, "I'm such a loser" can instantly turn into, "I have lost." "I'm an idiot," can be changed to, "I've done some silly things at times."

Do not think that because these distinctions are so subtle they don't have powerful effects over the way we feel toward ourselves and others. Words mean a lot! I have been on a "search and destroy" mission for *always* and *never* for many years, and I can personally vouch for the success in instantaneously draining the negative charge out of an emotional state with this simple, easy shift in language.

Two words you should always remember never to use.

*"So, like a forgotten fire, a childhood can always flare up again within us."*

GASTON BACHELARD

# Soothe Your Inner Child

I have a confession to make that is a little embarrassing, but here it goes: I sometimes cry at movies. When I was a kid I shed tears during certain episodes of *The Brady Bunch*, and might still do so if I watched them again! When I became an adult, I noticed that I cried during movies too, and even when listening to sentimental songs.

Now I don't mean to say that I cry during the most recent installment of *Batman* or some doomsday flick. I can deal with that stuff just fine. For me, it's the tender dramas about dysfunctional families (*Ordinary People*), the love stories (*Ghost*), you know, deeply emotional stuff that tugs at the heartstrings.

We all have many parts that make up who we are. The part of me that cries during movies is the little boy who resides inside of me and feels the pain of the character who is suffering the emotional hurt or the broken heart. My Inner Child is not only the source of much of my emotional outpouring during movies, but it also has a major role in some of my deepest wants, needs, desires, and creative energy. When he is not getting what he feels he needs emotionally, he lets me know in no uncertain terms.

Many adults did not have their emotional needs met adequately as children. They suffered from some combination of abuse or neglect, or conditional love, the kind of love that comes with strings attached. They didn't get enough, or perhaps any, unconditional love, acceptance, nurturing, protection, or emotional support. This feeling of *lack* can follow them throughout life, wreaking all kinds of havoc on their emotional well-being: anxiety, depression, insecurity, incompleteness, and a whole host of other negative ramifications.

If you feel this applies to you, take comfort in knowing that it's *never too late to love and nurture your Inner Child.*

Think of someone who loves you, or who once loved you, *no matter what.* If you can't think of anyone in your past or present, imagine what it would be like *if there were such a person.* You don't have to have a mental image of that special someone, just be aware of the essence of their love and their warm embrace. What we are about to do is have a written dialogue between your Inner Child and that person who sees you through the Eyes of Love.

Perhaps there is a subject that bothers you that involves your Inner Child crying out inside. Let's say, for instance, that you are worried that someone you care about is upset with you, or doesn't approve of you enough, or doesn't give you enough credit for all that you do. Your opinion about that person might, in fact, be true. In other words, maybe they *don't* give you enough credit.

What we're focusing on is how much their lack of approval bothers you deep inside, above and beyond what is in the realm of run-of-the-mill disappointment. While you are entitled to stand up for yourself when someone in your life is dropping the ball on your reasonable expectations, this exercise is geared toward those *unrealistic* expectations that come from the part of you that might be too emotionally sensitive or "needy."

To perform this exercise, write out a dialogue between your Inner Child and the one with Eyes of Love about a specific incident when the

Inner Child felt rejected. Let the child get it all out, no matter how childish, petty, whiny, or silly this might make you feel. Then watch as the one with Eyes of Love comforts the child with compassion and understanding while maintaining integrity by telling the truth.

Suppose the specific incident is that someone you love, and who you know loves you, has openly disapproved of something you have done.

*Inner Child: It hurts so bad! I thought she loved me and now she's rejected me. I need her to love me.*

*Eyes of Love: She does love you, sweetheart. Sometimes we hurt people we love. Love doesn't always feel tender and gentle. Rest assured, you are loved. And remember this; it's okay to want her to love you. That's only natural, but let's not go too far and say you always need her approval. Believe me, you would survive without it.*

*Inner Child: When will she prove to me that she loves me again? I don't want to lose her forever. I do love her. She seems so mean sometimes.*

*Eyes of Love: Honey, I can't answer that for you, but we both know that she loves you and she always will. She could have been in a hurry or in a bad mood. Her mood may have had nothing to do with you at all. We'll never know for sure.*

*Inner Child: I'm afraid. What have I done? She hates me now. She'll leave me and I'll be alone.*

*Eyes of Love: You're guilty of being human, that's all, and a beautiful one at that. She knows that, and I do too. I don't know what would make you think she's going anywhere else. She's never said that and she didn't say that she hates you either, so let's stick to what we know. It'll be alright, I promise. Just keep talking to me, whenever you want, about whatever you want. I will love and support you, no matter what happens.*

Go back and forth for 5 or 10 minutes or however long it takes, until the Inner Child has expressed every single worry or complaint they can think of. Make sure Eyes of Love has addressed every last concern like a loving parent would calm a child. In this make-believe world, Eyes of Love always gets the very last word. You'll know you are finished when the Inner Child has nothing left to say, and has gone to sleep for the night.

Soothe your Inner Child.

*"I don't think of all the misery but of the beauty that still remains."*

ANNE FRANK

# Sift Through the Pain to Find Some Meaning

*"The day that my miracle son, Paul, was diagnosed with a major, permanent, and irreversible disability, including severe mental retardation, my world came crashing down around me. He was 13 months old. We had gone through great lengths to "save him" while still inside my uterus. And he had survived! Although intuitively I had known that things were not quite right with Paul in his first year, having my fears confirmed was absolutely devastating to me and the rest of our family."*

*I refer to Elizabeth Kubler-Ross and her five stages of grief in dealing with death, tragedy, or catastrophic loss, namely...*

*Denial, Anger, Bargaining, Depression, and finally...Acceptance.*

*I can say that these feelings accurately describe what I experienced upon learning of Paul's disability. I would not experience the physical death of my son, but rather the death of a dream, of hopes and a life that my son would never have, and that we could never have together as a family.*

*The process of complete acceptance of my son's condition took 10 years, once I was satisfied that myself and others had done all that was humanly possible to try to change Paul's situation for the better, and acknowledged that Paul's condition was not under my control.*

*And after the long and weary battle and the passing of the storm, came the peace. I can now say that Paul, despite the continued hardships involved in his care, is a blessing in my life. Paul has given me strength, tolerance, patience, spirituality, and above all an unbelievable amount of love."*

These are the poignant words of a dear friend, whose beloved son, welcomed into the world with great promise and anticipation, entered this world with an unknown malady that left him profoundly mentally disabled, unable to speak, and prone to autistic-like behavior. My friend was ultimately forced to resign herself to the realization that she will never hear him utter the words "I love you Mommy" and she suffered mightily through the painful process of adjustment that culminated in acceptance. Amply equipped with grace and equanimity, she has been able – somehow – to find meaning and peace.

Anyone who lives long enough will experience some sort of emotional pain, grief, or sorrow that befalls them or someone they love. Even those who have largely been spared severe adversity recognize that somewhere in the world a child is starving or suffering at the hands of an abuser, a woman is being raped, or a hostage tortured. A man learns he has terminal cancer; a wife finds out her husband has Alzheimer's; a teen is diagnosed with diabetes. Sudden death of a loved one, disability, and natural disasters are all things we hear about, read about, and for many, directly experience.

In my field of Maternal Fetal Medicine, seeing parents having to cope with the news that their child will never fulfill any of the hopes and dreams they had for him ensures them a lifetime of challenges punctuated by chronic sorrow. Why did this happen to us? To him? What did we do to deserve this? This can't be happening!

Pain is an inevitable consequence of living. Some of us appear to glide by with very little while others seem to have a target on their back for life's injustices. We can never know for sure why this is. The question then, is what do we do about it? How do we cope?

We must turn inward to find the answers. Whereas many people find these answers within their religion, others are compelled to reject religion at precisely these trying times as a response to their anger with a God who would allow this to happen. Regardless of whether pain compels one to embrace or reject religion, neither person is right or wrong, for the source of our answers is unique to each of us. Finding your answer to the pain of life's injustices might take some time. Despite being grounded deeply in her foundation of faith, it still took my friend ten long years to assimilate and accept the facts behind the cruel hand she was dealt! Fortunately, there is no rush, as no clock is ticking, and no one is counting the minutes until an answer is found.

The first step is not to ask for an immediate answer, but rather to give yourself all the time you need for one to appear. To do this, you must learn to wait.

Wait until the initial shock has passed and you are ready to find meaning. Wait until you have accepted that the facts of the matter can't be taken away, that the pain cannot be removed, but only transcended. Wait until you have at least a tiny speck of hope that even in the face of horrible adversity life is still worth living.

When you are ready, the key to meaning lies within the questions you ask, not in the answers. In a strange but magical way, the answers are embedded within those questions. The secret is that you must be willing to ask the right ones.

Why? Why me? Why him? Why her? These are the completely understandable questions, the ones we are automatically programmed to ask. It's okay to ask them, and I'm not suggesting that you stop asking them, but these are the questions that arise out of suffering. These are the *unanswerables* that yield no inner tranquility and promote no healing.

At some point, though — today, tomorrow, next year or well beyond — taking a leap of faith that hope and spiritual healing are possible requires asking some new questions. The starting point for asking these new questions begins with the belief in one simple statement. This belief will not take away the pain, yet it holds the promise to transcend it so that you can find some tincture of peace. What is this basic belief?

*Within every bad situation, a gift can be found.*

How odd to say this. What *gift* can possibly come from a mass murder or suicide? How can anything *good* have come out of the Holocaust? Where can a nugget of gold be spotted in raising a child with mental or physical disabilities, or God forbid, both?

The answers lie within the reflection produced within us by the circumstances. Bad things don't happen to produce the gifts that come of them. We obviously wouldn't seek out tragic circumstances, and would do everything in our power to avoid them. But when the unavoidable happens despite our best efforts, at some point we have the potential to look beyond the pain for the beauty that can come out of it. We need to ask ourselves:

"Where can I find the blessing in this?"

"What good has come out of it?"

"How has this hardship changed me for the better? Has it made me more patient, grateful, understanding, and giving? Has it helped me better accept myself or other people?"

"Whose entrance into my life as a result of this circumstance has been a treasure to me?"

The answers to these questions can be hard to find. They might be hidden beyond the suffering that envelops you. You might not want to look for them, or even believe they could possibly exist... at this point in time.

You can always look to others for inspiration to open yourself up to an attitude of discovery:

*The actor in the wheelchair with the fresh spinal cord injury creates a foundation to raise millions of dollars for spinal cord research.*

*The father of the murdered child devotes his life to solving missing child cases, thereby saving other children from a similar fate.*

*The young girl in hiding from the Nazis writes one of the most widely-read accounts of life under siege that touches the hearts of millions of readers for decades to come.*

*The outpouring of love and support from strangers helps those who have fallen victim to a devastating hurricane.*

*The everyday unsung heroes that insist their disabled child's life matters, even when their own hopes for them have been dashed a thousand times.*

These are but a few of the kinds of human achievements that deserve our respect and admiration. More importantly, these are the sorts of responses that answer the question, "What meaning can come out of life's unfairness?"

When we find meaning for our painful experiences we re-write the story we have been telling ourselves. While this doesn't make up for the suffering — nothing can — it can help us let go of at least some of the pain so that we can live more freely. Because it is never too late to re-write our stories, the promise of turning a tale of tragedy into one of hope and re-birth never goes away. For it is our *interpretation* of the event that holds the key for us to look beyond the suffering and find peace.

Finding the meaning does not change the facts of the matter, but within this meaning lies the potential, at least, to look beyond the suffering toward the reality that enduring hardship is itself an achievement, one for which you can stand proud and witness the suffering with the knowledge that, despite the inexplicably unjust tragic circumstances that you feel you don't deserve, your life has meaning. Not just in spite of the pain but *because* of it.

Sift through the pain to find some meaning.

# JOY

*"Life is not measured by the number of breaths we take, but by the moments that take our breath away."*

UNKNOWN

*"The possible's slow fuse is lit by the imagination."*

# What If You Were Already the Kind of Person You Wish to Be?

Many years ago, I accidentally fell asleep wearing my contact lenses. Generally this wouldn't be a problem if certain precautions had been taken prior to trying to remove them. I didn't know about those precautions at the time, but I most certainly do now! At the very moment I pulled on the dry, stuck, synthetic material, I immediately felt a searing pain in my left eye unlike any I had experienced before. I was in agony!

I didn't bring up this story to illustrate the fact that a corneal abrasion, the medical term for what I had just done to my eye, is excruciatingly painful. I mention it because of how I responded to the pain. Instinctively I rubbed my eye trying to remove something that wasn't there, but each time I rubbed, *the rubbing just made the pain worse.*

We all have ideas about what we want to bring into our lives and what we want to remove from them. We have a whole host of problems we would like to eliminate. The same holds true for negative emotions; when we feel them, we want them to leave as soon as possible. We don't want to feel nervous, unhappy, depressed, angry, addicted, and the list goes on. Anytime we focus on what we *don't want*, it's like rubbing the painful eye and expecting it to feel better, when in reality rubbing simply makes the pain much worse. The truth of the matter is focusing on getting rid of what we *don't* want works against us.

Let's say right now I asked you *not* to picture a big, beautiful juicy orange. Okay, go ahead.

I'm betting you noticed that the harder you tried not to think about what you didn't want to think about – the orange in this example – the more you actually *did* think about it. The same goes with our problems. The harder we think about *not* having them, the more we focus on them, and hence the worse we feel. It's as if the problem becomes a "goal," and we know from personal experience that the more we think about our goals, the more we are drawn toward fulfilling them. So, be careful what you ask for!

Think about it. If you walked around all day saying, "I don't want to feel miserable," what would you then do? Perhaps without even recognizing it, you would mentally see yourself looking miserable, and you would start to feel that way. You might then think that these feelings came out of the blue, but they didn't. You unwittingly created them when you focused on telling yourself, "I don't want to be miserable."

The good news is that just as negative images create negative feelings, positive images create positive feelings. The trick is to stop focusing on what you *don't* want and think about what you *do* want instead. Here are some examples of turning the negative into a positive:

"I don't want to feel anxious," really means "I want to feel more relaxed."

"I don't want to feel alone," really means "I want to feel comfortable being on my own."

"I don't want to feel bored," really means "I want to feel some excitement."

After you have formulated your *don't wants* into *do wants*, turn the rest of the job over to your imagination and play make-believe. Close your eyes and play a game called, "What would it be like..."

What would it be like if I could feel relaxed?

What would it be like if I if I could feel comfortable being on my own?

What would it be like if I could feel excited?

*What would it be like if I were already exactly the sort of person I wish to be?*

The beauty of using your imagination is you do not have to believe anything with strong conviction, only that what you imagine is "possible." Getting into the habit of playing make-believe with possibilities for just a minute or two at a time here and there, can actually change the way you see yourself. And once you see yourself as being a certain way, you literally feel and act as if you are that person, right now, and in doing so *you can feel absolutely amazing.*

What if you were already the kind of person you wish to be?

*"The secret of happiness is to admire without desiring."*

CARL SANDBURG

# Ease Your Cravings With a Simple Word

Many great thinkers, some religions, and a plethora of popular authors have directed seekers of happiness to cut themselves free of all attachments. This means giving up both needs and desires, and just living in the moment, enjoying the Now. Those who espouse "no attachments" would say, "Don't be dependant on anyone or anything outside yourself. Give up all your desires and you will be happy."

Have you ever tried this yourself?

I have tried my hand at completely letting go of all my attachments and frankly, this hasn't worked very well for me. I used to feel kind of inadequate for being unable to adopt this popular philosophy as other people claim to have done. Since that time I have taken what has been for me a more realistic approach in my attitude toward attachments, one that doesn't require devotion to any extreme principle. It is based on giving up thinking of attachments as an "all-or-nothing" scenario, and adhering instead to the more moderate principle of "balance."

Let's say we tell ourselves that we "need" something in our lives in order to feel happy, satisfied, content, whatever. If we currently don't have it, we're left with a void, a sense of incompleteness. The more we focus our attention on this void, the more frustrated we feel as we come face to face with our unmet needs.

Besides *needing*, we also desire or *want* things that we do not currently have, such as love, appreciation, money, and perfection. I suspect that practically everyone conjures up desires for more than they currently have, introducing a noticeable distinction between what they "want" and what they currently "have." The more wanting and the less having, the greater degree of yearning for more. The seeds of frustration have thus been planted!

Give up all your attachments? Really? Seriously?

If you can do this, then all the power to you! If you have tried and have been unsuccessful like me, I'll share with you the way I have dealt with the issue of unmet needs and desires.

Attempting to give up your attachments in their entirety is unnecessary, and in my mind, too extreme. Plus, having some attachments — to friends and loved ones — can actually enhance your sense of well-being and promote feelings of happiness. The conclusion I arrived at is based on *loosening* the attachments, as opposed to eliminating them. Once again, we rely on the immense power of words to create a subtle shift in what we say to ourselves which has a profound impact on how we feel.

An elegant solution to softening overpowering attachments is to sprinkle your vocabulary with the generous use of the word *prefer*. Substitute "I need more money" with "I would *prefer* to have more money." Replace "I want more appreciation" with "I would *prefer* to receive more appreciation."

I admit that *prefer* is a rather simple, unexciting word. If *favoring* or *rather* feels more attractive to you than *prefer*, give one of these a try the next time you say to yourself, "I need more..." As long as you embrace the spirit of softening your cravings or demands, feel free to use your own creativity in choosing your words.

Ease your cravings with a simple word.

*"If you only have a hammer, you tend to see every problem as a nail."*

Abraham Maslow

# SEE YOUR PROBLEMS IN A WHOLE NEW WAY

As a specialist in diagnosing birth defects, I spend a lot of time performing ultrasounds on pregnant women. Thousands upon thousands of times I have run a small ultrasound device over a pregnant belly to study every nook and cranny of an unborn baby's body. I wish science would put me out of business by rendering birth defects obsolete, but unfortunately it has not.

The most challenging part of the body to study is the heart. Unlike the stomach, kidneys, and brain, the heart is constantly beating and the shape is extremely complex, requiring several different views at different angles with varying degrees of magnification. Viewing it too closely can actually hinder the exam. To compound the difficulty, the unborn baby frequently changes its position, moving around in the process.

The trick to getting really great pictures is to constantly move the ultrasound device around the mom's belly at various angles and magnifications to capture the perfect image in a fraction of a second. This requires flexibility on my part, as the window of opportunity can close rather quickly. If I can't see the heart how I want to with one approach, I must shift quickly to find another that works.

Similar to performing an ultrasound, the problems that we face in life are often best viewed from multiple angles and distances until we discover the best approach to dealing with them.

Everyone has problems. Some people's are more plentiful than others and more severe, and resources to deal with them vary between individuals, but rest assured that we all have them. Many problems can be overcome; others are seemingly or actually insurmountable. One person may find it possible to rise above terribly difficult, intractable problems, whereas another may have trouble coping with what appears on the surface to be a trivial issue, but for that person can be like having a monkey on their back. Our biggest problems can be super-challenging and painful, and in the worst cases they bring us to our knees in surrender.

The difficulty that our challenges present is compounded if we *think* we have a limited repertoire of responses to deal with them. When we try to approach a particular challenge one way using the only method of dealing with it that we know and that doesn't work, then what? The answer may lie in seeing the issue in a whole new way. Just as I can change the way I look at a baby's heart on an ultrasound, you can adjust the way you look at a challenge. Changing the way you look at it can't change reality, but it can *change your perspective* in a way that opens the floodgates to creative solutions for overcoming or accepting it.

Think about a specific challenge in your life. After you finish reading this paragraph, in your mind's eye, see it face to face. Imagine shifting the image so you are looking at it from the side — a different angle than before. Next, pretend like you're looking at it from behind as a mere observer.

Did you feel different about this challenge when you *saw* it from a different angle? If yes, make a mental note of that. If not, have no worries, as not everyone has the same experience when seeing their particular situation from another viewpoint.

In a moment, imagine floating up into the air to look down on the challenge from above. As you keep floating higher and higher, perhaps you can see the problem getting smaller and smaller, until it appears very tiny from your new bird's-eye view. Close your eyes for a few seconds and try this.

Did you feel a little bit of emotional relief as you gained some *distance* from the problem?

Sometimes we see our problems in vivid color, making them appear real and alive. Such liveliness creates the illusion that it is a living, breathing entity that has staked out permanent territory in our lives. How different would you feel if you could see this challenge in black and white? Try doing that now with your eyes closed.

Did that ease the emotional impact on you in any meaningful way?

Seeing a problem from different points of view has the potential to dramatically lighten its emotional impact on you, literally freeing you up to approach it with a cool, calm, and collected mind. And as soon as you enter this space of detached clarity, the once-static, immovable "problem" that may have seemed invincible is no longer so; it has become a dynamic "challenge" that calls upon you to draw from your vast reservoir of creative resources to either overcome or accept it. To determine which one, we are wise to take refuge in the oft-quoted *Serenity Prayer*, attributed to Reinhold Niebuhr, whose enlightened counsel serves as a fitting reminder of our need to surrender to a Higher Power for the guidance to meet life's demands.

> *"God, grant me the serenity,*
> *To accept the things I cannot change;*
> *Courage to change the things I can;*
> *And wisdom to know the difference."*

See your problems in a whole new way.

*"Every artist dips his brush in his own soul, and paints his own nature into his pictures."*

HENRY WARD BEECHER

# UNLOCK YOUR CREATIVITY

I'm just going to say this up front: Everyone is creative. Not everyone believes it, though. How about you? Do you think you are creative? If not, I have some good news for you that I'm hoping will spark your creative imagination.

I'm not going to give you a pep talk about how special or creative you are. What I would like to do is let you in on a not-so-little secret I learned about creativity. If you'll give me a chance and hear me out, I think you might appreciate what I mean. What I'm about to tell you has to do with the link between creativity and natural talent.

Consider for a moment that any natural talent is a form of *intelligence*. A person can be intelligent in academics — "book-smart" if you will — but have no clue about how to relate to other people on an emotional level, meaning that they're lacking in emotional intelligence. Another person can have several intimate, satisfying relationships, yet have accomplished a limited amount of success in school. Many different types of intelligence or "smarts" exist, but the presence of talent in one domain doesn't in any way guarantee the presence of any talent in another. People can have natural abilities in athletics, music, dance, writing, math, public speaking, listening, persuading, teaching, "common sense," and many other areas, but no one is gifted in everything.

When we attempt to flex our creative muscles in an area in which we don't have much natural ability, we often fall flat. That is not to say that we can't improve our skill in say, painting for instance. Skills can be improved in virtually any endeavor, but creativity flows most easily from those areas where we find our natural intelligences.

Years ago, someone suggested I try my hand at screenwriting. This seemed like a great idea at the time. After all, I had a passion for movies, was able to see the "big picture" of a story, and possessed an analytical mind that could easily wrap itself around the concept of story structure. Plus, I possessed a natural affinity and enjoyment for learning new things. This idea seemed like a "no-brainer."

I first prepared myself for this enormous task, as I poured through book after book, studied classic and contemporary movies scene by scene, and took copious notes that highlighted all that I had learned. I jotted down my original story ideas and made story outlines. I scoured the library and bookstore to stimulate my mind for plot ideas. On paper, at least, I had mastered a new craft… until I actually tried to write a screenplay. That is when my troubles started.

Nothing I did seemed to prepare me to write a high-quality script. Oh sure, I could have taken a course or read more books, and at some point I'm pretty sure I could have become *better* than I was when I started, but in terms of creativity as a writer, I felt like a dud. If someone had asked me then and there if I were a creative person, I would have said, "No way." I felt that I did not possess a creative bone in my body. Passion, alone, was not enough to foment my creativity. Something else was missing.

Later on I realized what that *something* was.

I'm probably not creative in terms of writing screenplays, but that doesn't mean I'm not creative in other areas, extremely creative in fact. For clues about where to focus my efforts, I took inventory of those areas that come easy for me, so easy that I almost missed them as fertile ground ripe for the picking. As an example, I have always been creative at picking out presents for others. I love surprising people with untimed, unexpected gifts that contain a "Wow!" factor. This is only one small example, but it serves to illustrate just how creative and full of life I feel when it is time to pamper someone with "just the right gift."

What sorts of activities are you particularly masterful at?

Maybe you have talent in the area of music, public speaking, gardening, writing, athletics, or math. Think of the subjects that came most easily to you in school. If you think you have no natural ability to do anything, *think outside the box*. Look at qualities that you might feel are *negative*, but are talents nonetheless, such as debating, arguing, detecting imperfections, and pleasing others. Focus your attention on things you may do as effortlessly as breathing, even those you don't distinguish as talents such as listening or making friends.

Wherever your genius overlaps with your passion, this is the place to mine for creativity. Chances are there is more than one of these places inside of you, but one is all you really need to let it flow. Visit this place often. Imagine how you can manifest your natural brilliance in a way that will serve the world, even if it's just one person at a time.

Unlock your creativity.

*"Let yourself be silently drawn by the stronger pull of what you really love."*

# Do What Makes Your Heart Sing

"Wait for a bite!" the dad shouted to his young daughter. The little girl reeled her line in once again only to find an empty hook. Just moments before, tired of watching the plastic red and white fishing bobber float peacefully on the surface of the water, she grew impatient, and pretended to do all the things that real fisherman do. She yanked the pole fiercely from side to side and reeled in the fishing line, finally dislodging the last of her bait.

Waiting is no fun. Even worse, it can be a bore. Time seems to go by so slowly as we wait in line at the bank or post office. We wait for traffic to move in front of us. We wait for the oblivious driver of the red van to take his sweet time backing out of his parking space so we can nab it for ourselves. We wait to find our next project, one that inspires us. We wait... and we wait... and we wait!

Like the little girl who went fishing with her father, we get tired of waiting for the pull so we start to push. We try to force things to happen, even at the risk of going home empty-handed. We'll do anything — *anything* — but wait.

This *pull* that I am referring to is that first magical twinkle of inspiration that zestfully compels us to move toward something that really turns us on, beckoning us to "come-hither" as we are drawn like a magnet to play a new game purely for the sake of playing it. And we know deep down that we must seize these moments right away or the muse will evaporate just as surely as the snowflake that has ended its flight as it hits the ground.

But when the fish aren't biting, when we can't find something to do that turns us on, what is there to do? Where do we go looking for the next big thing to add flavor to our lives?

A while back I had this very problem. I was feeling a little bored and looking for some excitement, and couldn't think of a project or activity that really got my juices flowing. So, I ventured out to take myself on a "date." I went to the place I often go to search for ideas: the local Barnes and Noble. I have always loved big bookstores, if nothing more than to browse around seeing what new offerings are on display. On this particular day, I decided not to stick solely to my usual sections, but rather to expand my horizons to any subject that caught my fancy in any section of the store. I was looking for ideas, not books!

I decided to play a little game.

I walked through every aisle of the bookstore just to collect books whose covers drew me in on an emotional level. With thousands of books to choose from, I could ill-afford to start reading the inside of each one, so I let my gut instincts decide which books to pick up. After some period of time — I'm not sure how long — I had collected merely 10-15 books out of this entire mega-store, for Round Two of my perusal. I placed my stack down next to a soft, comfortable chair and sat down for a spell. Each one of these books, culled from diverse sections of the bookstore, had spurred my initial interest on a purely emotional, rather than intellectual, level.

I ended up purchasing two of them. As for the others, I wrote down their titles for future use. I also recorded the particular quality that each book possessed that led me to choose it. Each of these qualities, I quickly realized, were all ones that had gotten me interested in particular books in the past, and therefore, I reasoned, probably would do so again in the future.

One book I purchased depicted a new, innovative technique for baking artisan-style bread. I have always enjoyed cooking, so I wasn't surprised to find a cookbook in my possession. After a quick stop at the grocery store, I enthusiastically gathered what I needed to bake my first recipe, and from then on I was hooked! I ultimately experimented with making a wide variety of loaves, bought another bread baking cookbook, and have since given away dozens of loaves of warm, freshly baked bread characterized by a firm, crunchy crust, and soft inner crumb. This one simple exercise evolved into a new passion for baking bread that I have since enjoyed time and again, and so, hopefully, have the recipients of my gifts of bread.

If the fish aren't biting in your life, reel in your line and seek out another pond. Invite yourself on a date looking for that next whiff of inspiration. Take a trip to a bookstore, music store, or a hobby/crafts store. Page through magazines and clip out pictures that pique your interest. Surf the Internet. Talk to friends. Learn how to create a Vision Board. Someplace there will be a pull for you, a new *something* that turns you on, and when you find it, reel it in slowly.

Do what makes your heart sing.

*"To take wine into our mouths is to savor a droplet of the river of human history."*

CLIFTON FADIMAN

# Savor the Moment

So much of our lives are centered on "doing." *Doing* is vital to living in this world, to bettering our lives, supporting our families, and achieving our goals. In short, *doing* comprises a big piece of our lives!

Do you ever spend time immersing yourself in the pleasure of just "being?"

*Being* is the act of non-doing, occurring within the private space outside of time, insulated from the hustle and bustle of everyday activity. *Being* exists only for the sake of itself, whose afterglow prompts the utterance of seemingly trite little statements that people often make when they are feeling happy.

"It's the little things in life that matter."

"The best things in life are free."

We have countless ways available to us to enjoy the sensuous pleasures that the world has to offer. How easy it is to forget how to enjoy them, to ignore them, become numb to them, stop caring altogether, or to perceive that there is not enough time left over for "that sort of thing." When we have temporarily lost our ability to enjoy these "little things," the act of regaining our focus need only begin with the tiniest effort to seize these moments and reclaim them, if only briefly.

Savoring slowly for one minute at a time, in fact, is a wonderful place to start. Only one *slow* minute is all it takes to send a message to the world that you are still alive. Find some delicacy to savor very deeply for just one *slow* minute. That's all you need to start. Here are some singular moments to delight in:

- Take four deep and easy breaths through your nose.
- Taste your favorite flavor on the back of your tongue.
- Submit to the invigorating moisture of a hot shower.
- Indulge in the satisfaction of a job well done.
- Enjoy the crispness of cool, clean air.
- Wrap your arms around another warm body for a comforting hug.
- Inhale the fragrance of an early spring flower.
- Listen to the softness of a sweet melody.
- Savor a tall glass of cold, fresh water on a hot summer day.
- Give thanks with a grateful heart.

Savor the moment.

*"A thing of beauty is a joy forever: Its loveliness increases; it will never pass into nothingness; but still will keep a bower quiet for us, and a sleep full of sweet dreams, and health, and quiet breathing. . ."*

JOHN KEATS

# Catch and Release

Memories of warm summers nights in my hometown make me think of fireflies. Those mysterious glowing insects were kind enough to hover so peacefully in full view, trusting us to hold them gently in our hands to have a careful look. We often placed these amazing creatures in glass jars so that we could gaze at them longer and appreciate their immense beauty up close, finally releasing them back to nature when we'd had enough, and they had too.

Every single moment of every day possesses countless opportunities to borrow from nature a few moments of sheer beauty and amazement, only to release them back to their source when we are finished refreshing our souls. We can always relish the sweet fragrance of a blossoming lily, stand in awe at the majestic brilliance of a sunset, delight in the early morning song of a nightingale, and witness the love of a mother's tender caress.

Must we be blind to the everyday miracles that are swept into a heap of lost treasures?

Whether these moments last a few seconds, a minute, or an hour is beyond our dominion. One thing is for certain: these are but fleeting moments in the course of our day that give us much-needed refuge from the appointments we must keep, the bills we must pay, and the sometimes cruel fragments of everyday reality that beg for a sign that we are part of something bigger. However great or small, all forays into times of joy are fleeting, rendering them all the more precious and worthwhile.

Like the firefly, these moments are plentiful and accommodating to our slow-footed attempts to catch them. Yet they will slow down for us just enough that we can borrow them for our glass jar and enjoy them while they are in full glow. And like the firefly caught in the jar, we must not overstay our welcome, for there is work to be done, and the exquisiteness of these moments can only exist in contrast to those which are not.

Catch and release.

*"All things share the same breath — the beast, the tree, the man. . .the air shares its spirit with all the life it supports."*

CHIEF SEATTLE

# "Breathe In Peace, Breathe Out Love"

One day I received a letter from an acquaintance of mine whose signature was followed by this beautiful quote of unknown origin: "Breathe in peace, breathe out love." Always being on the lookout for fresh insights and new tools to add to my toolbox, I decided to try this out as a form of meditation. All I can say is, "Really cool!"

Whether sitting or lying down in a comfortable place, driving in my car, or even while walking around any old place, I simply take in a breath while thinking the word "peace," followed by letting out the breath *even more slowly* to the word "love." The out-breath is extended slightly longer than the in-breath since a prolonged exhale enhances relaxation. I like to breathe in and out naturally through the nose, rather than the mouth, but you can find out what works best for you. Try it yourself.

"Peeeaace…"
"Looooovvvvve…"

"Peeeaace…"
"Looooovvvvve…"

Continue for several breaths.

If you feel like *adding some color* to this very relaxing time-out, then you can literally do so. Think of a color that means Peace to you and imagine in your mind's eye that the color you've chosen is flowing through your nose and down into your lungs, permeating all the cells of your body.

When you breathe out, imagine the color of Love flowing out of you. It could be the same or a different color than that for Peace. As these breaths continue, allow the color of Love to surround you, gradually filling up the space around you, bathing you in this feeling as it grows.

I personally prefer the simpler way, using just the words without adding color. I encourage you to try it both ways and discover whichever way works better for you. That's what this book is about, doing what works for you!

You can enjoy this in a quiet moment, perhaps while lying in bed in the morning or at bedtime, or when you are on the run during the day — whenever you feel like taking a relaxing break. What a delightful way to take time out to soothe your soul.

"Breathe in peace, breathe out love."

*"We've got this gift of love, but love is like a precious plant. You can't just accept it and leave it in the cupboard or just think it's going to get on by itself. You've got to keep watering it. You've got to really look after it and nurture it."*

JOHN LENNON

# TEND TO YOUR GARDEN

With proper care and handling, the amaryllis bulb produces a spectacular, bell-shaped flower that stays in bloom for just a brief period of time before gradually withering away for the season, until the cycle repeats itself. Within the amaryllis bulb dwells a seed of hope that holds the promise of a future reward, just as the caterpillar foretells its metamorphosis into the richly-colored butterfly. Without adequate sustenance, no flowers can be expected. But when left in capable hands that have resolved to gracefully accept months on end of unrequited love, one can rightfully expect that the ideal amount of water, ample sunlight, and generous rotation will combine to achieve the desired result of amazing beauty that begs to be fully appreciated. Each new season of giving brings an even larger plant and a greater number of flowers.

In many ways, our most precious relationships require conscientious and meticulous cultivation, too, if we are to experience the various colors and hues of their flowers in full bloom. Many weeks can go by when the rewards we derive from a most treasured bond are not so spectacular, yet we know that failure to provide consistent nurturing can lead to a withering away of the life force that sustains it, threatening its very existence. Take the time to nurture your most intimate relationships with your loved ones. Do not take them for granted, telling yourself that, "They already know how I feel about them." I can almost guarantee that unless you say the words out loud, they may forget that you do indeed care for them.

Say, "I love you" to someone who matters to you. Write a love letter or send a card.

Cook a favorite meal. Enthusiastically read to a child, or gently massage some tired shoulders.

Pay close attention to someone special, enveloping them with your full and undivided attention for as long as they wish.

Dish out a well-timed hug, a warm smile, or a cold drink.

Ask a loved one how best you can serve them. You might be surprised at what you don't yet know.

Give the gift of *receiving;* allow a loved one to nurture *you* when they feel the need to give, and tell them all your favorite ways to be loved, for they might not know for sure.

The amaryllis pays you back in magnificent fashion but once a year. You don't heed its life-sustaining demands merely to receive its generous display of beauty for a brief measure of time. Most days, you do it out of pure love, from a place where giving is its own reward, and you expect nothing whatsoever in return. In time, when all is said and done, the results can be breathtaking!

Tend to your garden.

*"We can only be said to be alive in those moments when our hearts are conscious of our treasures."*

THORNTON WILDER

# GO FIRST FOR THE LOW-HANGING FRUIT

When I lived in the southern United States during my medical training, I used to love driving out into the country to pick my own peaches at a local orchard. The reason that fresh, hand-picked peaches are so much sweeter than store-bought peaches has to do with their shelf life. The ones intended for the stores are picked too soon because they must last longer to prevent spoilage, whereas the peaches left longer on the tree have more time to increase their sugar content, thus making them taste sweeter.

The first time I visited this grove, I noticed several people standing on ladders, stretching to reach the fruit hanging from the highest branches. I couldn't figure this out. After all, there was plenty of beautiful fruit on the lower branches within easy grasp. Despite the fact I had no fear whatsoever of heights, I just didn't see the point of stretching myself, of risking a fall and slowing myself down, when gorgeous, plump, ripe peaches were practically staring me in the face!

In life, we often think the fruits of success hang high up in the trees, so high that many times we don't even bother climbing. In reality, there is plenty of fruit right in front of us all the time, but for some reason we don't notice its presence. People who feel blue or depressed, in fact, may even have trouble seeing any fruit at all!

There is an expression that goes, "Happy people think a lot about what they have; unhappy people think about what they don't have." Most of us probably divide our time in various proportions thinking about some combination of both. What's interesting, though, is when we assume that only *after* our mood improves, *only then* will we begin to appreciate what we have. That may be true, but I have found that the reverse is at least equally true. When we begin to be grateful for what we have first, our mood improves as a consequence.

Defining people as being happy versus unhappy, as if you are a member or non-member of an elite club, does not appear to me to be either accurate or useful. It seems to me that a more valuable and authentic way to phrase this expression is to say, "People feel happier when they think thoughts about what they do have in their lives than they do when they think excessively about what is missing."

Appreciating the gifts you have, especially when you feel down in the dumps, can seem like an exercise in futility. That's not to say you don't "know" what you have on an intellectual level, but experiencing true gratitude for your good fortunes, the kind that you feel deep inside, can seem to rest high up on the top branches out of your reach. The answer then is to go for the low-hanging fruit.

Many books have been written about the numerous benefits of incorporating habits of gratitude into your life. For me, when life is going well, it's easy to feel grateful, but during some tumultuous period of life, feeling grateful, even with the help of exercises to foster those feelings, may be easier said than done. During those times, waking up every day and counting my blessings in my head may occasionally have given me rushes of mood elevation, but after a while I found myself making mental checklists of items for which I should be grateful, and it became a chore, devoid of the fruit of a grateful feeling. In theory, practicing gratitude habits to enhance appreciation for life and brighten my day makes a lot of sense. Theory and practice, unfortunately, are not always in alignment.

In practice, when I've been in a positive emotional state, feelings of gratitude have been pretty easy to come by. Learning to induce them from a negative emotional state, however, has often made me feel like I was staring forlornly up at those tree-top peaches without a ladder anywhere in sight! Fortunately, there is always the low-hanging fruit to get us through the rough patches.

Some people benefit from writing regularly in a Gratitude Journal. Scientific studies have even shown a psychological benefit of sitting down *once each week* and making a list of things for which one is grateful, yet this approach is not the only way to engender feelings of gratitude. What works most easily and effortlessly for me — and I am hoping for you — is the low-hanging fruit, which is something quite different from making a list. It is based on the idea that *acting* grateful will cause *feelings* of gratitude to bubble up inside of you. In other words, demonstrating gratitude will help you feel grateful. When you want to express your gratitude and appreciation, you go right to the source. Here are some suggestions that you can modify using your own remarkable creativity and life circumstances:

Write a letter to someone you love, to express how you feel about them and what they mean to you, even if they already know! Don't hold back.

Send a thank you note or greeting card to those who have contributed to your life — friend, teacher, caretaker, clergy, shopkeeper, business owner, and especially a loved one — expressing in great detail how much they have meant to you.

The next time you have an attentive server at a restaurant, ask to speak to the manager, and compliment the server right in front of them!

If you believe in God, say a sincere "Thank you" on a regular basis for the many gifts that have rained down on you from high above.

Decide for yourself what best works for you. Choose the kinds of activities that will stir your inner sense of gratitude and expand your will to share it. The list of possibilities is infinite!

Go first for the low-hanging fruit.

*"A bit of fragrance always clings to the hand that gives you roses."*

# DELIGHT IN THE GREAT JOY OF GIVING

*An elderly Jewish couple is sitting together on an airplane flying to the Far East. Over the public address system, the Captain announces:*

*"Ladies and Gentlemen, I am afraid I have some very bad news. Our engines have ceased functioning, and this plane will be going down momentarily. Luckily, I see an island below us that should be able to accommodate our landing. Unluckily, this island appears to be uncharted; I am unable to find it on our maps. So, the odds are that we will never be rescued and will have to live on the island for a very long time, if not for the rest of our lives."*

*The husband turns to his wife and asks,*

*"Esther, did we turn off the stove?" and Esther replies, "Of course."*
*"Esther, are our life insurance policies paid up?" "Of course."*
*"Esther, did we pay the money we pledged to the United Jewish Appeal?"*
*"Oh my God, I forgot to send the check!!"*
*"Thank Heaven! They'll find us for sure!!"*

This joke is emblematic of the importance of charity in the Jewish faith, as is true in essentially all major religious faiths. Whether our contributions are in the form of time, money, or possessions, and whether we give to individuals, communities, specific organizations, or in response to natural disasters, we are all called to give.

Giving is a two-way street. We give what we can to benefit others mostly because we feel that we are morally compelled to do so, but that does not diminish the effect that our generosity has on ourselves, the givers. Feeling wonderful about ourselves for giving is not selfish; it appears that our Creator cast us this way to energize the habit of giving, which is advantageous given the frequency with which we are inundated with requests. Here are a few of the ways we are called upon to contribute:

- The child who rings our doorbell pitching support for their local team.

- The hastily-convened celebrity telethon to aid victims of the latest natural disaster.

- The bone marrow drive to find a perfect match for the leukemia-stricken teen.

- The book fair to raise money for the community library.

- The annual charity drives to feed the poor, comfort the sick, and provide meals for the elderly.

- We are asked to save the whales, the rainforests, and endangered species whose names we've never even heard before now.

Even the most generous and compassionate among us cannot give to every cause and every person. Possessing an enormous capacity for love and compassion for others doesn't translate into an infinite amount of money, time, and energy to meet more than a small fraction of our requests. At some point we must decide to whom, how much, and by what means will we transfer our abundance. Do we base our decisions solely upon obligation, personal interest, or even guilt? For I believe that many of us have, at one point or another, been driven by all three.

I am not suggesting that you exclude any opportunity for giving back. If you feel compelled to make that annual contribution, support your house of worship, or sponsor the local baseball team, by all means continue.

I *am*, however, making a pitch for you to include in your stockpile of choices a certain kind of giving, the kind that feeds your own spirit, in addition to the beneficiaries of your largesse.

Whether you give your money, time, or possessions, no one can decide what is right for you except you. Whatever ways of giving you choose, be on the lookout for those special rare opportunities that irresistibly draw you in for reasons you can't explain, other than the fact that they bring you great joy. Giving from the heart can involve giving money, but it often involves giving your time; time that you might not feel you have left over from the demands of everyday life; time that you would somehow need to "create."

What can you give when you don't have the time to mentor a child, volunteer in a soup kitchen, or serve a meal to the elderly or infirm?

Multiple opportunities present themselves for us to demonstrate compassion and kindness to strangers, acquaintances, and friends alike. Some of my greatest pleasures have come from helping others in the most unexpected ways, from scenarios that have popped up out of nowhere and wreaked havoc in the lives of others. Sometimes my own giving has involved trusting the other with my own personal safety, which required a delicate exercise of judgment to be sure. Such examples of unplanned, heart-felt giving are:

🦋 Stopping to help a stranded motorist

🦋 Giving much-needed cash to a co-worker displaced by a house fire

🦋 Providing counsel to a relative who is depressed

- Visiting a bereaved widow, long after many of her friends have stopped calling
- Providing a senior citizen an arm to latch onto as they cross the street
- Taking a lost dog to a shelter
- Picking up the tab for the police officer sitting at the table next to you
- Sending a card to a teacher, doctor, or member of the clergy, thanking them for their service
- Hand-delivering a lost wallet to its grateful owner
- Calling the parents every anniversary of their son's death
- Taking time to listen to someone who is lonely
- Thanking a member of the armed forces for their sacrifice
- Sending a warm smile to someone who is "down and out"

I bet you can think of numerous, even innovative ways to give in your own style, on your own terms, to someone who could use your help. Every day some chance to give, however small it may seem to you, will come your way. You need no special occasion at all; just a loving desire to lift someone's spirits.

Delight in the great joy of giving.

*"In the world to come, I shall not be asked, 'Why were you not Moses?' I shall be asked, 'Why were you not Zusya?'"*

Rabbi Zusya

# LIVE FROM YOUR HIGHER PURPOSE

For many years, through different seasons of my life, I heard the Call for Meaning in the form of the question: "What on earth am I here to do?" Sometimes the call was very quiet, almost imperceptible, whereas at other times it stared me directly in the face, demanding an answer, and creating a generous amount of existential angst. Once I finally came face to face with my own unique truth, I was able to stop searching and just relax. Funny how the answer was inside of me the whole time.

What are you here on earth to do? Perhaps you already know. If that is true, consider yourself fortunate, one of the lucky few. If you don't have any idea, you're in good company.

Purpose is not a job or a career, though it can be expressed through one. It is not a goal or a destination. It is not something that is created out of thin air.

Your purpose is already known, and your task is simply to discover it. Once you do, you will recognize that it forms the fabric of your being; the starting point that informs everything that you do; the place from which you come to lay your unique contributions like a wreath of flowers onto the world.

Some people can state their purpose with little thought. Others need to explore and contemplate this for weeks, months, or even years. As for me, it took years, many years, to discover my purpose.

It may be that discovering your purpose is actually a matter of remembering. Why do I say "remember?" Because I believe that deep down, on some level, we all know what our purpose is, and through the trials and tribulations of life we have forgotten the answer on a conscious level. Once we remember, we find that living in congruence with our life purpose is one of the cornerstones of a meaningful life, opening the door to transforming any ordinary experience into an extraordinary one.

We are so designed that abundant creativity springs forth from our natural endowments, and because this is so, access to our own personal treasure trove of ideas for expressing our purpose is never far away. It is the way we are designed. And so it will be with you when you discover *your* higher purpose, if you have not already done so.

Your past – your life story – is littered with scattered clues as to what is your purpose. The formula for inching closer to your purpose is to scour your past to collect these often subtle clues – like turning over oddly-shaped pieces of a jigsaw puzzle to discover how they fit together – to build a portrait of who you truly are. The key to success is finding the right combination of incisive questions to zero in on the answers that identify the essence of your life's meaning.

When in the past have you felt most "alive?"

What sorts of things have consistently turned you on or have put you in "the zone," activities that you have chosen and would choose again in a heartbeat, merely for their own sake?

What were you doing at the time you experienced an unusual amount of happiness or bliss?

How would you enjoy spending your time if you were wealthy beyond a shadow of a doubt?

What is the most satisfying way for you to contribute to the well-being of others?

Once I was able to articulate a one-sentence expression that depicts my own life purpose, one whose focus gave my life meaning, I found myself engulfed in a special sort of peace that comes from walking on hallowed ground. All the paths leading away from this sacred place are well-appointed and easy to follow. No more drifting around in the morass of an arid desert, as I had once done year after year. From this special place flows at once the desire to love and commit to others and the blueprint for doing it.

Every day I ask myself, sometimes more than once, what can I do to live from my purpose? And because this is *my* purpose, I greet each day equipped with those natural proclivities endowed to me by nature, gifts that I neither asked for nor earned, but for which I am eternally grateful.

Before I tell you my life purpose, I'd like to first help you lay the groundwork for discovering your own life purpose because this book is not about me, it's about *you*.

Whenever you have the time and emotional space to contemplate, such as in the morning when you first awaken, or while lying in bed at night, ask yourself, "What on earth am I here to do?" Open yourself up to receiving an answer. Each time you hear the faint whisper of an answer begin to form in your mind, write it down in a journal or notebook, even if you're not sure that it will lead you in the right direction. At some point, in a week, a month, or years, look back over all that you have written and begin to put the pieces together, so that you, too, can articulate your life's meaning in a single sentence or two. At that point, you can begin to ask a different question each day for the rest of your life, one that is much easier and much more fun, to answer, namely, "How can I manifest my purpose today?"

My higher purpose is to *fill the hearts of others with* **Comfort, Healing, and Joy**.

# About David Fox, M.D.

**David Fox, M.D.** is a specialist in Maternal Fetal Medicine, expert in personal growth and development, Master Practitioner of Neuro Linguistic Programming (NLP), experienced meditator, award-winning teacher, hypnotist, black belt in Tae Kwon Do, avid cook, and long-distance runner. Dr. Fox graduated summa cum laude with a degree in philosophy from the University of Cincinnati, where he was inducted into Phi Beta Kappa. He earned his medical degree from The Ohio State University. He lives in Columbus, Ohio.

To learn more visit
**www.ComfortHealingandJoy.com**

LaVergne, TN USA
17 February 2011
216934LV00005B/15/P